The Micro-Historian's Guide to
RESEARCH, EVIDENCE, & CONCLUSIONS

Step-by-Step Research Planning & Execution

for Historians, Genealogists, Journalists, Museum Professionals, Specialty Researchers, & Local History Enthusiasts

by Reginald W. Bacon

ROWMAN & LITTLEFIELD
Lanham • Boulder • New York • London

Published by Rowman & Littlefield
An imprint of The Rowman & Littlefield Publishing Group, Inc.
4501 Forbes Boulevard, Suite 200, Lanham, Maryland 20706
www.rowman.com

6 Tinworth Street, London, SE11 5AL, United Kingdom

Copyright © 2018 by Reginald W. Bacon

All rights reserved. No part of this book may be reproduced in any form or by any electronic or mechanical means, including information storage and retrieval systems, without written permission from the publisher, except by a reviewer who may quote passages in a review.

Typography note: The body text and chapter headings in this book about history research are purposefully set in Helvetica, an unadorned sans-serif typeface that exudes a rugged modernity. The typeface, designed in 1957 by Max Meidinger (1910–1980) based on late-19th-century German/Swiss neo-grotesque designs, has become the most commonly-used sans-serif typeface in the last 50 years. Originally licensed to the Linotype Corporation for hot metal composition, in the 1960s the typeface was adapted for photo-typesetting systems, resulting in a proliferation of clones. In the 1980s, Helvetica was licensed to Adobe and Apple, and was bundled with the first wave of laser printers. Today, Arial, a 1982 "adaptation" by a 10-person team at the Monotype Corporation, is a ubiquitous Helvetica derivative. In 2007, a documentary film and museum exhibition commemorated the 50th anniversary of Helvetica. The variety of fonts in the Helvetica family make it one of the most versatile typefaces, expressive in nuance from a whisper to a scream. Helvetica remains all around us, on corporate logos, business forms, online, in print, and on rest room doors. Versions used in this book are from the Bitstream Corporation's "Swiss 721" typeface family licensed and released in 1982.

British Library Cataloguing in Publication Information Available

Library of Congress Cataloging-in-Publication Data

Library of Congress Control Number: 2018905458

ISBN 9780997752847 (cloth) | ISBN 9781538137390 (pbk) | IBSN 9781538137406 (electronic)

Table of Contents

Introduction 5
Acknowledgments 9
Research Planning 11
- Formulating the Inquiry
- Building a Foundation of Context
- Surveying & Prioritizing Sources
- Planning for Efficient Source Exploration & Documentation

Research Execution 27
- Gathering Information On-Site & Online
- Keeping a Research Log & Documenting Sources
- Allowing for Improvisation & Serendipity

Evaluation of Evidence 37
- Evaluating for Substance, Relevance, & Reliability
- Deriving Facts from Evidence
- Understanding Proof Standards & Proof Levels

Formulation of Conclusions 49
- Objectivity and the Limits of Knowledge
- Historiography & Interpretation
- 21st Century Microhistory
- Change, Continuity, & Causality

The Summary Narrative 73
- Conceiving the Narrative
- Historical Writing: Descriptive, Narrative, & Analytical
- Outline & Organization
- Writing the Summary
- Editing & Proofreading

Parting Thoughts – Timeless & Timely 91
Appendix I: Local History 101 93
Appendix II: Genealogy 101 99
Appendix III: Source Citation 101 103
Bibliography 105
Index 109
About the Author 112

The Micro-Historian's Guide to
RESEARCH, EVIDENCE, & CONCLUSIONS
Introduction

Research: Digging for the 'stuff' of history
Primary Souces ~ Secondary Sources ~ Material Objects
Environmental ~ Geographical ~ Spatial ~ Evolutionary ~ Biological
Agricultural ~ Technological ~ Political ~ Sociological

New stuff & 'now' stuff ... on the surface
Future history researchers will navigate mountains of print and electronic sources ... or perhaps a potholed landscape of missing sources if electronic records are lost in the digital netherworld due to accident, neglect, or intent.

Studies in 21st-century microhistory:
Narrow observational scale • Focus on ordinary lives
Focus on small social units • Focus on a single period or locale
May focus on one sociological, economic, cultural, or technological topic
Includes methodology & commentary • May or may not link to macro-history

Relatively new stuff – 20th century

Traditional 'great man' history: Hagiographic • Focus on power elite

19th-century old stuff…& really old stuff
Thanks to 19th-century technological advances in communication (printing) and transportation (distribution), tangible sources proliferated that benefit historians of today.

Studies of history in ancient times:
Historians of ancient times relied on sage elders who told heroic stories of their civilization's triumphs.

Ancient stuff

Prehistoric stuff

Studies of pre-history:
The study of pre-history by scientists of all disciplines has illuminated understanding of human history on many fronts.

Introduction

In years of public presentations for history enthusiasts, tours for museum visitors, consultations for research clients, and conference sessions for professionals, I have eagerly responded to requests for advice on research methods, reliability of sources, and evaluation of evidence. In my view, sharing what I have learned along the way is "paying forward" the guidance received from countless librarians, archivists, and curators of generous spirit encountered in my own research travels. In your hands is this "paying forward" – expanded, formalized, and finally sandwiched between the covers of a book.

Rationale. *The Micro-Historian's Guide to Research, Evidence, & Conclusions* imparts useful guidance to motivated historians, genealogists, special-interest researchers, and local history enthusiasts. As long-buried sources become available via the internet, more regular folks without a Ph.D. in history are joining in the fun of information-gathering and shining new light on under-explored history – yet often with no foundation of method. This book ramps up the fun, and answers the need with a compact and straightforward overview of the foundational theory, practice, procedures, and standards of professional research and evidence analysis. The aim is to help the new history practitioner build a foundation of research skills that leads to evidence-based conclusions.

Microhistory. This book addresses and inhabits the realm of *microhistory*, the genre of interpretive history that seeks understanding through the study of ordinary lives and under-the-radar subjects. At best, it is the "micro" investigations within a given topic that lead to an elevated understanding of the "macro" big-picture history of that topic. The sub-specialty of microhistory coalesced in the latter decades of the 20th century as a refinement – or methodological offshoot – of the "new social history" approach to historical interpretation. The first wave of micro-historians found that some large-scale quantitative studies by their social science colleagues arrived at generalizations that were at odds with the up-close reality of the ordinary lives from which they sought to draw universal conclusions.[1]

The Micro-Historian's Guide to
RESEARCH, EVIDENCE, & CONCLUSIONS   *Introduction*

Early microhistory scholars such as Carlo Ginzburg (b. 1939) and Laurel Thatcher Ulrich (b. 1938) narrowed their observational scale, and focused their studies on small units and relationships within individual social settings. An earlier standard was set by George R. Stewart (1895-1980), with his 300-page description of a 20-minute battle in *Pickett's Charge: A Microhistory of the Final Attack at Gettysburg* (1959). The works of Stewart, Ginzburg, and Ulrich still stand out as masterful examples. Ginzburg's *The Cheese and the Worms* (1976) tells the micro-detailed story of a Menocchio [Domenica Scandella (1532-1599)], an ordinary miller brought to trial during the Inquisition and executed in 1599. Ulrich's *A Midwife's Tale* (1990), the real-life-as-lived story crafted from the diary of Martha Ballard (1735-1812), a midwife in rural Maine, won the Pulitzer Prize in 1991.

In the last 20 years the best-seller list has been routinely populated by general-audience books with a sociological or technological microhistory component. Perhaps the best-known is *Cod: A Biography of the Fish That Changed the World* (1997) by Mark Kurlansky (b. 1948). His books on salt, milk, and paper followed, which encouraged other ambitious scholars to research and write comprehensive, engaging micro-histories on everything from beer to bananas.

To the avid local historian or family genealogist who may have tuned out of history way back in the 8th grade, understandably stupefied by a fusillade of dry-as-dust names, dates, and served-up "facts," it may come as a welcome reassurance that there is far more to our human history than just generals and wars. Fortunately, out there to be chronicled by historians are the gamut of chalk-talkers and chocolatiers, prostitutes and proslytizers, screwdrivers and screwballs. There is no shortage of raw material.

Organization & content. The foundation of method is presented in five sections: (1) Research Planning, (2) Research Execution, (3) Evaluation of Evidence, (4) Formulation of Conclusions, and (5) The Summary Narrative. Subsections break down the method for easy understanding of the developing process. Each major topic is enriched by practical examples from personal experience that take the reader behind the scenes of the historian's craft.

It is important to note here that the foundation of method advanced in this book is not intended to be a confining straitjacket. The step-by-step method is intended to be more like a set of training wheels. Among the real-world examples are instances of serendipitous discoveries made possible by following a "hunch," breaking free from the research plan, and exploring blind alleys. As many a fellow

The Micro-Historian's Guide to
RESEARCH, EVIDENCE, & CONCLUSIONS *Introduction*

jazz player has learned through hands-on experience, one's improvisational creativity is ultimately based on one's instrumental mastery. That mastery is the solid foundation of one's craft attained only through disciplined repetition and practice. In any craft, the basis of *freedom* is *discipline*. So it goes with the craft of research. Build your foundation. Be disciplined. Have a plan. Master your craft. And then you will know when and how to improvise down those blind alleys.

This book's amalgamated content draws theory from, and pays tribute to, dozens of history, genealogy, historiography, and research notables through the ages, including (in alphabetical order): Robert Charles Anderson; Wayne C. Booth, Gregory G. Colomb & Joseph M. Williams; Fernand Braudel; Donn Devine; Val D. Greenwood; Herodotus; Martha Howell & Walter Prevenier; Donald Lines Jacobus; Carol Kammen; Ibn Khaldun; Dom Jean Mabillon; David McCullough; Elizabeth Shown Mills; Leopold von Ranke; Barbara Tuchman; Thucycides; and others. Recommended writings of these giants and near-giants are included in the bibliography.

This foundation of method is packed with the italicized terminology of the research process. Other books, other experts, and other systems might define terms differently, or use different terms altogether. But more important than memorizing specific definitions is understanding the research process. When you understand the process, you can think like a researcher – which is one of the aims of this book.

Point of view. This book is informed not only by my research experience for books, articles, consultations, exhibitions, public programs, and conference presentations, but by the totality of three separate but interrelated careers: investigative journalist and editor; performing artist and scholar of early 20th-century music, vaudeville, and circus; and museum professional with specialties in 17th-century New England architecture and domestic life. The perspective of experience, especially as a no-nonsense old-school newspaper reporter and editor, occasionally prompts a good-natured tease of the buttoned-down genealogy proof standard, a deflating poke at puffed-up historical interpretation, or an editor's snarl at flabby academic writing.

Appendices. The book includes three appendices that serve as introductions to local history, genealogy, and source citation. The first two appendices are adapted in part from my own previous publications on the respective topics. Much of the content of Appendix I: Local History 101, is drawn from insights gleaned while working on *A Micro-History of the Tannersville Four-Corners (2011)*, a social, cultural, and economic history of a small town in the High

The Micro-Historian's Guide to
RESEARCH, EVIDENCE, & CONCLUSIONS *Introduction*

Peaks region of New York's northern Catskill Mountains. The content of Appendix II: Genealogy 101, is adapted from an introduction to genealogy of the same name prepared for experiential "walk in the footsteps of ancestors" programs at New England historic house museums (2005-present). Appendix III: Source Citation 101, presents the principles of source citation, with examples of formats from the *Chicago Manual of Style* (17th ed., 2017), the *MLA Style Manual and Guide to Scholarly Publishing* (8th ed., 2016), and *Evidence Explained* by Elizabeth Shown Mills (3rd ed., 2017).

Topical bibliography. The bibliography includes the following categories: historiography, general history theory & practice, local history theory & practice, genealogy theory & practice, the craft of research, source citation, and the craft of writing. As a self-directed learning resource, the bibliography expands the modest 112 pages of this book to thousands of pages of wisdom from the masters.

Parting thoughts. The foundation of method is followed by a chapter of selected parting thoughts, a catch-all of observations, tips, warnings, and exhortations. The dozen parting thoughts were conceived as pithy reminders of *timeless* principles relevant to the topics of research, evidence, and conclusions. But during the course of assembling this book, circumstances have pushed these best practices, especially those related to the evaluation of evidence, to a front-and-center position that has made them *timely* as well as *timeless*. In this era of disparagement of the free press, assault on truth-seeking scholarship, threats to freedom of speech, and a national crisis of failing media literacy, all of our citizens, young and old – not just wanna-be historians – might benefit from a refresher course on research, evidence, and conclusions. The long-established principles of evidence evaluation advanced in this book align almost exactly to the most up-to-date principles advanced in media literacy education, and as such may be more *timely* than ever.

My hope is that this compact guide proves useful to those who value evidence-based discoveries. May *your* research yield a fortune of priceless insights to share. To those who embrace the principles and ideals within this volume: Go forth and multiply! Happy reading.

                                  – Reginald W. Bacon
                                     Newburyport, Mass.
                                           July 2018

(1) Carlo Ginzburg. "Microhistory: Two or Three Things That I Know About It." *Critical Inquiry 20* (Fall 1993). (Chicago, Ill.: University of Chicago Press, 1993), pgs. 10-35.

Acknowledgments

In this project, as in so many others, I have been fortunate to "stand on the shoulders of giants."

For a foundation in research, I still look back with gratitude to the journalism professors and editors who were the mentors and "giants" of my investigative reporter days, among them the late Ed Arnold, Bill Cahill, Cathy Covert, Paul Kenyon, and Elden Rawlings.

In my own realms of research, "giant" role models past and present include historians, genealogists, researchers, and authors who have set the bar high, among them Bernard Bailyn, Fernand Braudel, Barbara Tuchman, and Laurel Thatcher Ulrich (historiography); Alf Evers, Peter Benes, Abby Hemenway, and Carol Kammen (local/regional history); Abbott Lowell Cummings and James L. Garvin (early New England domestic architecture); Lynn Abbott, Doug Seroff, Arnold Shaw, and Loring H. White (music); Frank Cullen, Frank Wertheim, and Don B. Wilmeth (vaudeville); Janet Davis, Stuart Thayer, and William Slout (circus); and Robert Charles Anderson, Donald Lines Jacobus, and Elizabeth Shown Mills (genealogy).

A special thank-you is extended to the hundreds of libraries, archives, museums, and research repositories visited through the years – in person and online – that provided the opportunity to put into practice, and refine by trial-and-error, the system of research planning and execution advanced in this book. The welcoming, knowledgeable, and helpful librarians and archivists at such repositories are always the researcher's best friends.

Personal gratitude is extended to my select pre-publication readers who shared their combined accumulated judgment and expertise: Sharon Spieldenner (professional archivist and sought-after local history research adviser), Nicki Girouard, (history/museum colleague and scholar/researcher of New England Colonial-era history), and L. J. Newton (my wife, longtime stage performance partner, and ever-dependable tether to good sense ... and making sense).

A usage note ... from a historian: Yes, that's "a historian." Not "an historian." Let pronunciation be your guide. Use the article "a" before consonant sounds, as in "a historic house," and the article "an" before vowel sounds, as in "an old house." This may defy fusty academic convention, but this is the judgment of the author/historian who is also an editor. [See *Garner's Modern American Usage* (2003), pg. 1; and the *Chicago Guide to Grammar, Usage, and Punctuation* (2016), pg. 228.]

The Micro-Historian's Guide to
RESEARCH, EVIDENCE, & CONCLUSIONS *Research Planning*

A "Research/Evidence/Conclusions" Flow Chart

■ **RESEARCH** ■

Formulate a Research Inquiry
What's your curiosity? Use a research inquiry template.
Address the "Who cares?" and "So what?" questions.

Build Contextual Knowledge
Topical – Historical – Chronological – Geographical – Jurisdictional

Survey Relevant Sources
Narrative Sources (published & unpublished) – Diplomatic Sources
Social Document Sources – Archaeological & Material Sources
Primary Sources **(Direct & Indirect)**
Secondary Sources **–** *Tertiary Sources*
Evaluate potential sources for *Conditions & Intentions*.

Plan for Exploration of Sources
Plan for efficiency and practicality for on-site and online explorations.

Work the Plan – Gather *Information* from *Sources*
On-Site Sources – In-Person Sources – Online Sources
Thorough and accurate *Source Citation* is imperative!

— *No Short-Cuts This Way!* —

■ **INFORMATION** ■
Information is extracted from *Sources*, and is **Direct** or **Indirect**.

■ **EVIDENCE** ■
Evidence is derived from *Information*, then analyzed and interpreted.
Evaluate *Evidence* for *Substance, Relevance, and Reliability*.

■ **FACTS** ■
Synthesized *Facts* derived from *Evidence* build the *Rationale* for *Proof*.

■ **PROOF** ■
Assign proof level (Possible, Probable, Highly Probable, Almost Certain).
Proof Standards:
Legal/Deductive – *or* – Historical/Diplomatic – *or* – Scientific Method

■ **CONCLUSIONS** ■
Complete *Evidence*-based research summary or reader-focused narrative.
New Research Questions?! *Go back to the top!*

— *New research questions? Go back to the top … where the fun begins again!* —

10

Research Planning

Research planning? "Who needs a plan?" some might say. Why not just barge in, fire up the computer or phone, and start fiddling? Something interesting on the subject is bound to turn up, right? Well, for the curious mind, stumbling across random tidbits of history is fun and often sparks deeper interest. But once a casual curiosity becomes a focused historical or genealogical inquiry, the project will benefit from a research plan. In case anyone needs to be convinced about the value of having a plan, consider this timeless wisdom of Yogi Berra: "If you don't know where you're going, you'll end up someplace else."[1]

Research is our subject here, so the questions are: What is it? Why do we do it? Who does it? How do I begin? Where do I do it? What do I look for? And do I ever finish? These questions give shape to both the research plan and its execution.

What is research? *Research* is nothing more than the *process* of finding answers to solve a problem, clarify a curiosity, or explain a situation. The problem, curiosity, or situation can be of a practical nature for which the research findings result in a specific solution, or of a research nature for which the research findings result in improved understanding.

As for *who* does research, first coming to mind are the best-selling author-historians that enjoy the fruits of hard-earned reputations ... fortified with healthy advances from their publishers. Next to mind are the harried history Ph.D. candidates hoping their work leads to gainful employment. Then coming to mind are the undergraduates filling history course requirements on their way to a non-history, liveable-wage-producing degree. But in fact, non-authors and non-academics outside those categories frequently undertake some form of research, whether it is tracking down the online manual for the old microwave oven, digging out an old hard-copy magazine to refresh our memory of a classic 1956 Corvette, or visiting the library for any resources, old or new, that can help us make sense of the

The Micro-Historian's Guide to
RESEARCH, EVIDENCE, & CONCLUSIONS — *Research Planning*

latest national or global insanity. In recent decades, the unprecedented online access to all manner of sources has attracted to the field new waves of enthusiastic do-it-yourself genealogists and local historians "without portfolio."

As for *how* research is done, in the layman's examples like the ones mentioned above, we piggyback on the expertise, documentation, or previous research of others. The researcher with a plan, however, not only mines the published knowledge of others for context, but also has the fun of getting the hands dirty in digging for and evaluating primary source materials.

As for *where* to do research, it is the libraries, archives, and public record repositories – whether one visits them in-person or online – that are the obvious places to find primary and secondary source books, documents, and photographs. But *what* to look for in a research project may also include material objects, buildings, landscapes, audio/video recordings, art, in-person interviews, and more, scattered far-and-wide.

Does a researcher ever really *finish*? Research into the grand mess of history and human affairs, unlike research in the more predictable physical sciences, does not guarantee eureka!-like discoveries, ironclad conclusions, or earthshaking insights. A modest summary of inconclusive research, or even a prize-winning book of revelatory findings and new interpretation, may amount to a mere temporary historical "truth" until superseded by new research and interpretation five years or 50 years later. Therefore the historian must face the reality that almost every history research project, in some respect, amounts to a "summary-to-date."

Informing the research plan, execution, evaluation of evidence, interpretation, and summary is the researcher's own conception of history. The chapter entitled "Formulation of Conclusions" includes discussion of historiography and the various approaches to interpretation. The approach in this book aims to be most useful to the newcomer to the micro-history subset of the craft, but the elements of research planning and execution are applicable to information gathering regardless of the researcher's preferred theoretical scope.

The four elements of research planning are (1) formulating the inquiry, (2) building a foundation of contextual knowledge, (3) surveying and prioritizing the variety of sources relevant to the inquiry, and (4) planning for the efficient exploration and documentation of the selected sources.

Formulating the Inquiry

All research projects begin with a question to be answered or a problem to be solved. The first step, then, is to narrow the subject interest to a stated research goal. That goal might be to answer a specific question, discover a specific unknown, or prove (or disprove) a specific hypothesis.

Pulitzer prize-winning historian David McCullough has said in many interviews that "I try to write the kind of book that I would like to read." In other words, he is most motivated to research the topics he is personally the most curious about. "Sometimes I think I don't go after the idea," he has said, "but the idea comes after me."[2] Your project is most likely to succeed if it is infused with your passion to address your own curiosity.

When you are defining your "mental itch" that needs to be scratched, ask the "who, what, when, where, why (and how)" of the subject interest. One of those "five Ws" will jump out as the most compelling kind of research question. Then it is imperative to ask yourself – and objectively answer – the "So what?" or "Who cares?" question. This will help you nudge your research question from half-hearted interesting inquiry to a worthwhile question of a more broad significance.[3]

A simple template for a research inquiry might be expressed as: "I am researching _____ because I want to find out _____ in order to convey understanding of _____."

Some practical examples of formulating the inquiry:

• In formulating the research inquiry for *A Micro-History of the Tannersville Four-Corners* (2011)[4], the phrasing indicated the narrow, micro-focus on a small but constantly evolving geographical area: "I am researching this intersection in the small mountain town of Tannersville, N.Y. because I want to find out about all of its businesses and property owners from 1813 forward, in order to convey understanding of its evolution from a 'tavern at the crossroads' serving seasonal 'bark-peelers' of the early 19th century, to its late-19th-century 'grand hotel' era as a summer destination for sweltering New Yorkers."

• In formulating the research inquiry for the section of individual family profiles in *Early Families of Middletown, Connecticut, Vol. I: 1650-1654* (2012)[5], the phrasing was particularly broad: "I am researching each of the first 23 17th-century-settler families of

Middletown, Conn. because I want to find out their familial, geographical, occupational, economic, religious, and political relationships, in order to convey understanding of the growth and development of this second-generation colonial-era settlement."

• In formulating the research inquiry for John Henry Buckbee (1837-1890), one of the three research subjects in *Chauncey Richmond and "The Old Buckbee": The Story of a Banjo, Its Maker, and Its Player* (2018)[6], the phrasing addressed understanding the curiously growing popularity of the 5-string banjo among proper Victorian-era ladies in the 1880s: "I am researching John Henry Buckbee because I want to find out about the man behind what was once the largest banjo factory in the world, in order to help my reader better understand the expanding banjo market in the urban northeast U.S. in the 1880s."

In the fine reference entitled *The Craft of Research* (1995, 2003), the authors differentiate between what they refer to as *practical problems* and *research problems*. In scientific or public policy research, a *practical problem* caused by certain conditions and costs is addressed by *applied research* that can at best suggest a remedial action. In the realm of history and genealogy, a *research problem* – in which the condition is the lack of knowledge, and the cost of not knowing is abstract – is addressed by *pure research* that can illuminate our understanding. At best, however, even in an inquiry into a *research problem*, the understanding derived from *pure research* can also contribute to solving *practical problems*.[7]

Building a Foundation of Contextual Knowledge

Nobody is born knowing everything. We are all stupid about something. So unless you only research in subject areas in which you already know everything, a concentrated study of the context all around the periphery of your research topic is in order. Professional journalists must continually self-educate, as they may be reporting on cancer research one day, and doing a feature on African art the next day. It is essential for a real pro to be the master of where to go for authoritative context on a variety of subjects. You can be just as aggressive in pursuit of context. The first survey of sources will be in general reference works, then specialized references, then specific research guides and bibliographies. The bibliographies will lead you to relevant individual works and current scholarship on a subject or individual. In historical and genealogical research, knowledge of geographical and jurisdictional context of the regions you are studying can be just as important as the topical context.

Some practical examples of context acquisition:

• In context acquisition for *Chauncey Richmond & "The Old Buckbee": The Story of a Banjo, Its Maker, and Its Player* (2018), in preparing for research on John Henry Buckbee and his banjo factory, readings for context included not only all the relevant banjo scholarship, but the 19th-century history, geography, and development of the Tremont section of the Bronx. N.Y. where the Buckbee factory was located. In addition, the "FAN" approach (FAN = friends, associates, and neighbors) was utilized in studying decade-by-decade census records to ascertain granular contextual detail about family relationships, neighbors, and employees.[8]

• In context acquisition for *The Visitor's Guide to the Weeks Brick House & Gardens* (2015)[9], readings for context included all of the earliest surveys of New England domestic architecture, and then the more specific references on the region's earliest brick houses. This grounding in context informed the subsequent exposure and correction of prideful but unsubstantiated "first" and "oldest" claims about the 1710 brick house in Greenland, N.H.

• Context acquisition for *The HABS and the HABs NOTs: Documenting the Architecture of Newburyport in the Historic American Buildings Survey* (2017)[10] included immersion in historical, sociological, and economic sources in order to fully understand the protracted mid-20th-century economic malaise in the small coastal city of Newburyport, Mass. – an enduring depression of decades that preserved acres of the city's remarkable stock of early domestic architecture by the phenomenon of "preservation by benign neglect."

A caveat on context: Exploring context is essential, but there is a hazard. The interpretations within well-crafted secondary source histories consulted as context can be so on-point and convincing that they may, in stealth, close the historian's open mind ... or blunt the sharp edge of your own original research.[11]

Surveying & Prioritizing Sources

Sources for history research include everything and anything that informs the "who, what, where, when, why (and how)" of people and events of the past. That is, sources are not just the first page of hits on a Google search, or a single category of books in one section of the library stacks.

Sources may include all manner of archaeological sources: Artifacts including three-dimensional objects of material culture such as

The Micro-Historian's Guide to
RESEARCH, EVIDENCE, & CONCLUSIONS *Research Planning*

furniture, clothing, tools, art, crafts, musical instruments, structures, landscapes, and human-made infrastructure. A subset of this category includes printed ephemera, photographs, maps, diagrams, audio & video recordings, and oral histories. Most familiar in academic research are literary or narrative sources: Books, newspapers, magazines, unpublished texts, letters, diaries, databases, interview transcriptions, internet postings, online publications, and more. Also familiar is the category of diplomatic sources: Government records, court records, and legal documents. Related to this is a category familiar to genealogists, social document sources: Indices and records produced by government and non-goverment bureaucracies that include vital records (birth, marriage, and death), church records, business records, and organizational records.

All sources in the categories noted above can be further categorized as primary, secondary, or tertiary. Primary sources are texts, records, or relics created in the period. Primary sources can be either direct (created at the time and place), indirect (an inventory, bibliography, or compiled database of the time and place), or both (ex.: an inventory created by an individual at the time and place). Secondary sources include research, books, articles, or artifacts not created at the time and place, but which are instead based on primary sources. Tertiary sources include books and articles not created at the time and place, but based on secondary sources. Tertiary sources further interpret a subject, explain new research, or find new meaning from an array of secondary sources.

Because all sources are not equal, it is wise, for time efficiency, to survey the available sources relevant to the historical or genealogical inquiry before diving into them. Your survey of sources will help you make an efficient research plan for exploring them. (Don't worry, you will still have plenty of opportunities for wonderfully adventurous time-consuming sojourns down blind alleys.)

Locate the sources ... and prioritize for relevance. From your preparatory immersion in context, by this point you are already familiar with secondary and tertiary sources on your topic. Comb the footnotes and bibliographies of your context sources, and then use your framed research question(s) to identify the new-found sources within that are most relevant to your research. Use your well-honed research question(s) to engage the assistance of librarians & archivists. These professionals are your valuable allies in research.

Regarding hard-copy in-print sources and digitized sources via the internet: An original primary source in hard-copy will always be the preferred source over a digital copy, transcription, or compiled index. But of course access to the original is often impractical and sometimes impossible. Fortunately, with every passing day more digitized versions of reliable primary sources become available on the internet to view, print, and cite. The online digital collections of museums, libraries, and archives from the U.S. Library of Congress down to small-town historical societies are gold mines of historical and genealogical research sources. The digitization of newspapers continues steadily, and websites like *www.archive.org* (Internet Archive) provide free access to millions of digitized books, magazines, and ephemera, all in page images faithful to the original.

The contemporary researcher is wise to be mindful, however, of the hidden biases of digitization in index terms and database search algorithms. It has become a concern that the way digital archives are built and organized may unintentionally influence interpretation of research materials. Microfilm vs. digital newspaper research offers a good example: If searches of a digital database yield only individual articles instead of entire pages, the researcher misses out on the page-wide period context viewable on microfilm. In this example, the digital-only researcher may increase time efficiency, but at the expense of deeper contextual understanding. At the 2018 annual meeting of the American Historical Association, one panelist, at a session entitled "Primary Sources and the Historical Profession in the Age of Text Search," opined: "I think I'm writing history, but in reality the search engine is writing history because it's determining what I click on."[12]

Further, as we live through the growing pains of the great democratization of information enabled by the World Wide Web, we must constantly be aware that alongside websites with access to digitized sources of unquestioned reliability, are websites and blogs with no gatekeeper; mountains of uncurated, unedited dross; intentional misinformation; bald-faced bias; inflammatory distortions; and flat-out lunacy. The good news for researchers is that for some projects, the internet and its uncurated blogs, twitters, and chatters can also be primary sources for what people from all backgrounds and points of view are thinking and writing about a particular issue at a particular point in time.

Prioritize sources for reliability. Now that you have lined up and prioritized by relevance the sources you would like to explore, consider in advance their relative reliability. This is separate from evaluating the evidence you may eventually derive from information within the source. Granted, evaluating for reliability is sometimes impossible until you get deep into the source information itself, but prioritizing in advance as much as possible results in more efficient research.

When evaluating primary sources for reliability, consider the following: Is the source genuine, and accurately located in place and time? Is the source authentic, and not an intentional forgery or fake? Is the source an original or a copy? Is the source a combination of an original with subsequent additions? Is the source legible and comprehensible? Sometimes specialized knowledge is required to evaluate sources. The independent researcher is wise to build a network of professionals like handwriting experts, deed researchers, archaeologists, and genealogists.

When evaluating secondary and tertiary sources for reliability, consider the following: What is the likelihood of transcription errors in a clerk's copy of vital records? If the source is a book or article, was it published by a reputable press? Does the author of the source have a proven reputation for scholarship? Where does the source stand in the timeline of scholarship on the topic?

When evaluating sources accessible only online for reliability, be mindful of the caveat above about websites hosting uncurated blather that loiter in the internet neighborhood alongside websites of libraries, archives, museums, historical societies, and genealogical organizations that host reliable source material.

For all sources, a researcher must consider the conditions and intentions of the source at the time it was produced. For example, a memoir may have been written to intentionally recast history (intentions); or a structure may have been built as a garage (conditions) before it was transformed into a home and became the birthplace of your research subject. Conditions and intentions will also be part of the subsequent scrutiny of evidence.

Some practical examples of preliminary source surveys:

• In the preliminary source survey for *Chauncey Richmond & "The Old Buckbee": The Story of a Banjo, Its Maker, and Its Player* (2018)[13], to find out more about how small-town farmer Chauncey Richmond (1872-1910) succeeded as a vaudeville promoter and trolley park manager, primary sources created at the time and place included census records, vital records (birth, marriage, and death records), articles in newspapers and periodicals, maps, and photos. Secondary and tertiary sources included compiled government

The Micro-Historian's Guide to
RESEARCH, EVIDENCE, & CONCLUSIONS   *Research Planning*

reports, and books and articles about the 19th-century minstrel show era, early 20th-century vaudeville, and the development of trolley line amusement parks. In evaluating for source reliability, "conditions and intentions" came into play with the coverage of Lincoln Park activities in the *Norwich Bulletin*, as one co-owner and one board member of the newspaper were investors in the Norwich & Westerly Railway Co.

• In the preliminary source survey for *The Juggler's Manual of Manipulative Miscellanea: The Classic Skills with Top Hats, Cane, Plates, Nesting Cups, and Assorted Objects* (1984)[14], to learn the broad range of object-manipulation specialties performed in late 19th and early-20th-century European music halls and American vaudeville theatres, relevant sources created nearest to the time and place of performances included hundreds of detailed descriptive reviews published in newspapers and magazines. Secondary sources published years later included the monthly *Juggler's Bulletin* (1944-1949) and the *Juggler's Bulletin Annual* (1951-1953) both compiled and edited by Roger Montandon (1918-2017), that featured interviews with veteran performers recollecting the greats from earlier days. Montandon's publications were supplanted by The International Jugglers' Association *Newsletter* (1949-1981) and later magazines. But in this area of special interest research, it is the later secondary source publications that are higher on the reliability scale. This is due to the greater objectivity of the creators, who, to their credit in seeking factual information, cut through the relentless theatrical hyperbole of the early newspaper and magazine reviewers.

• In the preliminary source survey for *Vintage from Vinyl: Early Recordings of the Goodtime Ragtime Vaudeville Revival* (2017)[15], the goal was to fortify an already robust foundation of knowledge in late-19th and early-20th century popular music. To achieve this goal the most valuable sources were of a secondary nature – acclaimed compiled scholarship that had already corralled hundreds of relevant primary sources in footnotes and bibliographies. In turn, the primary sources were invaluable in the new book's several myth-bustings about the minstrel era, vaudeville, jazz, and early "hillbilly" music.

A caveat about the preliminary source survey: Be guided, but not confined, by the preliminary source survey. In *inquiry-based research* as described thus far in this chapter, the carefully-framed inquiry might suggests only well-worn sources to study, and therefore the researcher might miss out on outlying but valuable sources. Conversely, in its opposite, *source-based research*, in which the researcher hunkers down with a narrowly-focused group of sources and allows those sources to determine multiple winding paths of inquiry, that researcher may revel in the discovery of the outlying sources, but in the end have before them only a mountain of marginally-related data ... and a long list of unanswered research questions. But after years in the trenches of research, you will learn through experience – and through deep familiarity with sources within your specialties – that a side-trip departure to source-based research can be useful and productive.[16]

Planning for Efficient Source Exploration & Documentation

After you have identified, located, evaluated, and prioritized your sources, you can make the optimal, logical, time-efficient plan for digging into them for information.

For on-site visits to libraries, archives, museums, and other repositories of sources, it is the travel time and logistics; the open days and hours; and the availability of librarians, archivists, and curators that factor into planning. Today we have the convenience of almost instantaneous telephone and email contact with librarians and archivists to make advance arrangements. In addition, because so many research repositories today have online catalogs and finding aids for their holdings, researchers can determine in advance the call numbers for books, microfilm rolls, documents, photos, and other records. For in-person consultations or interviews, planning includes the location, schedule, format, and recording details as well as thorough preparation of questions. For tromping through cemeteries, poking around urban archaeology sites, or exploring more remote-but-relevant landscapes, each type of expedition will have its own planning requirements and gear from galoshes to gas mask. Good planning that is common to all on-site visits includes preparing your arsenal of documentation tools, from pencils, paper, laptop, phone, and a reliable camera with spare batteries. To ensure your own batteries stay charged for an extended period of top concentrative effort, make sure to pack food and water – not for chomping and slurping in the archives, but for your dash-outside breaks for personal refueling.

For online research, plan to explore the foundational census and vital records sources first, as your findings within those sources may suggest other research inquiries. Whether planning to execute your online research by source category, geography, period, or individual, try to sequence your work so you will not have to backtrack unnecessarily – like having to go back to the same census page a dozen times. This advice is derived from the author's years of repeated backtracking through census pages.

Thorough preparation includes planning ahead for the documentation of sources. Create a simple blank source documentation form – a database for your computer, a hard-copy form, source documentation software, or all three – for recording complete information about every source consulted, down to the book and page numbers. Using a source documentation form such as the one shown on the next page will make your life easier in the long run. Weeks, months, or even years later, when the time comes to summarize research or write a history or genealogy narrative, your collection of information-packed source documentation forms close-at-hand, in hard-copy or database form, will moderate the tedium of formatting footnotes and bibliographies. At this writing, the bible of source citation for historians and genealogists is *Evidence Explained: Citing History Sources from Artifacts to Cyberspace*, by Elizabeth Shown Mills (Baltimore, Md.: Genealogical Publishing Co., 2007), 885 pages of wisdom, theory, practice, and examples from the master.[17]

Some practical examples of research plans:

• The plan for researching John Henry Buckbee (1837-1890) for *Chauncey Richmond & "The Old Buckbee": The Story of a Banjo, Its Maker, and Its Player* (2018)[18], placed first priority on census and vital records. His Civil War service, in the middle of his chronology, was added to this first priority. The next priority was exploring map sources and local histories correlating to the census places. Third in priority was exploring sources related to his banjo-making craft and business, which included tax records, business records, city directories, newspaper articles, advertisements, maps, and musical instrument catalogs. The broad context that informed this plan was gained by prior immersion in secondary and tertiary sources by notable banjo history scholars. Online and on-site destinations included the Bronx (N.Y.) Historical Society, Brooklyn (N.Y.) Historical Society, Brooklyn (N.Y.) Public Library, The Gotham Center for New York City History, Museum of the City of New York Archives, New York City Municipal Archives, New York Historical Society, New York (N.Y.) Public Library, and the New York State Archives (Albany, N.Y.).

• The plan for researching the textual, visual, and verbal presentation content for *A Vaudeville Retrospective*[19] (2008-present), the illustrated lecture, performance, and traveling lobby exhibition

The Micro-Historian's Guide to
RESEARCH, EVIDENCE, & CONCLUSIONS

Research Planning

Researching an individual or topic: Use a source documentation form

Not to be confused with the research log explained in the next chapter, a source documentation form, in hard-copy or digital form, is an efficient way to record the necessary information for footnotes and bibliographies. The creative form-builder will design a custom form to meet the needs of individual projects or types of sources.

Source Documentation Form

Research Project: _____
Individual/Topic: _____
Page ___ of ___

Source: Book/Article/Record	Author or Creator	Publisher, Location, & Date	Page Numbers	Repository Location	Call Number	Date Accessed	Misc. Research Notes, URL, etc.

The Micro-Historian's Guide to
RESEARCH, EVIDENCE, & CONCLUSIONS　　　　*Research Planning*

exclusively for museums, historical societies, libraries, and college theatre departments that relates the history of American vaudeville 1880-1930, began with a methodical study of secondary-source scholarship. As a theatrical stage performer for 35 years, and as a researcher, author, and steward/keeper/teacher of my acrobatic juggling, physical comedy, eccentric tap, and jazz/ragtime musical specialties, my foundation of contextual knowledge about the history of vaudeville entertainment was already solid. The preliminary survey of sources, however, discovered more recent scholarship on vaudeville and related turn-of-the-20th-century popular culture. So it was essential, in conceiving this new history-based presentation upon my retirement from commercial showbusiness, that all scholarship, old and new, be revisited.

Based on the freshly-reviewed contextual knowledge, the illustrated lecture was refined into seven sections, from the introduction that properly defined the genre and addressed myriad misconceptions, to its late-19th-century beginnings, through its growth as an industry, through the economics of its 1930s decline, and its survival to the present in different forms. Each section would require its own engaging and relevant macro- and micro- stories of people and places – and illustrative visuals for digital projection. Therefore the research plan included digging into primary source texts suggested by the preliminary review of sources, and searching for accompanying public domain photos, illustrations, and printed ephemera. Newspapers like the *Brooklyn Daily Eagle*, the *New York Clipper*, and *Variety*, packed with performance reviews by knowledgeable scribes, were prime sources. To illustrate the stories of famous and forgotten performers, and of grand theatres and rickety outdoor platforms, repositories like the U.S. Library of Congress and the New York City Library of the Performing Arts supplanted a large personal collection of performer's publicity photos, postcard views of palatial theatres, street scenes with glowing theatre marquees, performer contracts, show programs, and posters, and other assorted ephemera.[20]

The research plan for the exhibition component of *A Vaudeville Retrospective* included consideration of three-dimensional objects, not just documents. An ongoing study of vaudeville-era juggling props, wardrobe items, prop trunks, and implements of a 1920 traveler's daily life informed the acquisition of authentic objects for display. The research plan for the performance component of the presentation was the easiest of all: Each performance segment would reprise a stage-worthy musical interlude, choreographed juggling piece, or acrobatic stunt from a 35-year vaudeville repertoire.

- The multi-year plan for researching individual social and cultural history topics in *Early Families of Middletown, Connecticut, Vol. I: 1650-1654* (2012)[21], placed first priority on coordinating and synchronizing travel time with the different open hours at a half-dozen central Connecticut research repositories. Advance planning for each research trip, about three hours from home, included the obvious concerns of vehicle prep; a stocked cooler of food-and-drink; hotel reservations; and fully-charged phone, laptop computer, and digital camera. Plenty of coins and dollar bills were stockpiled for parking meters and copy machines. Advance work online included consultation of finding aids at each repository's website, and then preparation of a list of sources to be studied at each. With much research already accomplished online, the aim of these research trips was to dig deeper into obscure document sources and material object sources not yet digitized. The schedule called for starting early, ending late, and visiting multiple libraries in the course of each research day. Separate notebooks-with-*pencils* (not pens!) were prepared for documentation of research on each of several topics. Topics included individual 17th-century families in Middletown; the indigenous people of the region; early domestic architecture in central Connecticut; the development of public services and public infrastructure; Puritanism in the second-generation settlement; land grants and property ownership; geographical and economic expansion; agriculture; crime; the beginnings of ship-building and maritime trade; and African-Americans and the slave trade in colonial-era Middletown. The plan called for transcription of critical hand-written notes and source documentation on the laptop computer back at the hotel in the evening. Spanning several years during editorship of *The Middler* (a publication devoted to the colonial-era history and genealogy of Middletown, Conn.), the plan called for multiple visits to the Connecticut State Library, Connecticut Historical Society, and the Connecticut Genealogical Society, all in Hartford, Conn.; and in Middletown, Conn., Godfrey Memorial Library, Russell Library, the Middlesex County Historical Society, and Olin Library Special Collections & Archives at Wesleyan University.

Were Yogi Berra and Abraham Lincoln teammates? At the beginning of this chapter was a relevant quotation by baseball great Yogi Berra on having a plan. And, yes, he was a Yankee. At the conclusion of this chapter, it is fitting to invoke a quotation often attributed to another heavy-hitter, Abraham Lincoln: "Give me six hours to chop down a tree, and I will spend the first four sharpening the ax." (While the wisdom is instructive, Lincoln never said it. Its origin is unknown.)

The Micro-Historian's Guide to
RESEARCH, EVIDENCE, & CONCLUSIONS — Research Planning

NOTES to Research Planning

(1) Yogi Berra with Dave Kaplan. *When You Come to a Fork in the Road, Take It!: Inspiration and Wisdom from One of Baseball's Greatest Heroes*. (New York, N.Y.: Hyperion Publishing, 2001), pg. 53.

(2) David McCullough, interview with Bruce Cole. "The Title Always Comes Last," *Humanities Magazine*, May/June 2003. (Washington, D.C.: National Endowment for the Humanities, 2003).

(3) R. W. Bacon. *The Cranky Editor's Book of Intolerable Fox Paws (Oops! Faux Pas!)*. (Newburyport, Mass.: Variety Arts Press, 2014), pg. 19-36 ("Fox Paw #1: Fuzzy Goals & Ill-Defined Purpose," and "Fox Paw #2: Weak Organization").

(4) R. W. Bacon. *A Micro-History of the Tannersville Four-Corners*. ((Newburyport, Mass.: Variety Arts Press, , 2008, 2011).

(5) R. W. Bacon. *Early Families of Middletown, Connecticut, Vol. I: 1650-1654*. (Newburyport, Mass.: Variety Arts Press, 2012).

(6) R. W. Bacon. *Chauncey Richmond and "The Old Buckbee": The Story of a Banjo, Its Maker, and Its Player*. (Newburyport, Mass.: Variety Arts Press, 2018).

(7) Wayne C. Booth; Gregory G. Colomb; & Joseph M. Williams. *The Craft of Research*. (Chicago, Ill.: University of Chicago Press, 2008), pg. 59.

(8) Elizabeth Shown Mills. *QuickSheet - The Historical Biographer's Guide to Cluster Research (The FAN Principle)*. Baltimore, Md.: Genealogical Publishing Co., 2012.

(9) R. W. Bacon. *The Visitor's Guide to the Weeks Brick House & Gardens*. (Newburyport, Mass.: Variety Arts Press, 2015).

(10) R. W. Bacon. *The HABS and the HABs NOTs: Documenting the Architecture of Newburyport in the Historic American Buildings Survey*. (Newburyport, Mass.: Variety Arts Press, 2017).

(11) John Tosh. *The Pursuit of History: Aims, Methods, and New Directions in the Study of History* (6th ed.). (New York, N.Y.: Routledge, 2015), pg. 156.

(12) Stephanie Kingsley Brooks. "Search History: Making Research Transparent in the Digital Age," *Perspectives on History* (March 2018). Washington, D.C.: American Historical Association, 2018), pg. 16-18.

(13) Bacon, *Chauncey Richmond and "The Old Buckbee": The Story of a Banjo, Its Maker, and Its Player*.

(14) R. W. Bacon. *The Juggler's Manual of Manipulative Miscellanea: The Classic Skills with Top Hats, Cane, Plates, Nesting Cups, and Assorted Objects*. (Newburyport, Mass.: Variety Arts Press, 1984).

(15) R. W. Bacon. *Vintage from Vinyl: Early Recordings of the Goodtime Ragtime Vaudeville Revival*. (Newburyport, Mass.: Variety Arts Press, 2017).

(16) Tosh, pg. 99-100.

(17) Elizabeth Shown Mills. *Evidence Explained: Citing History Sources from Artifacts to Cyberspace* (3rd ed.). (Baltimore, Md.: Genealogical Publishing Co., 2017).

(18) Bacon, *Chauncey Richmond and "The Old Buckbee": The Story of a Banjo, Its Maker, and Its Player*.

(19a) R. W. Bacon. *A Vaudeville Retrospective: American Vaudeville 1880-1930* (2008-present) (illustrated lecture, performance, & exhibition). *www.VarietyArtsEnterprises.com*.

(20) R. W. Bacon. *The Curator's Guide to American Vaudeville 1880-1930*. (Newburyport, Mass.: Variety Arts Press, forthcoming in 2019).

(21) Bacon, *Early Families of Middletown, Connecticut, Vol. I: 1650-1654*.

The Micro-Historian's Guide to
RESEARCH, EVIDENCE, & CONCLUSIONS — *Research Execution*

'Working the Plan': A Research Execution Checklist

On-Site Research

Travel & Logistics at Departure
___Transportation/vehicle prep
___Directions/maps/GPS to destinations
___Coins/cash/card for parking
___Hotel reservations & confirmation #s
___Cell phone & charger
___Weather check (for clothing/travel)

Advance Tools to Pack
___Library/archives schedules
___Library/archives contact info
___List of sources & call numbers
___List of research goals & questions
___Context charts, maps, notes, etc.

On-Site Tools to Pack
___Notebook, pencils, & pencil sharpener
___Research Log & Documentation Form
___Coins/cash/card to feed copiers
___Laptop computer & power cord
___Digital camera (& batteries)

Personal Supplies to Pack
___Water/juice/food/snacks/medicines
___Hand cleaner/sanitizer; toothbrush
___Positive attitude & sunny disposition

On-Site Information-Gathering
___Follow the house rules
___Make legible notes in pencil
___Photocopy documents if possible
___Print from microfilm reader if possible
___Fragile sources: Use an extract form
___Transcribe notes ASAP

Source Documentation
___Author/creator
___Title
___Type of work
___Publication place & date
___Page number, section, etc.
___Repository location
___Call number
___Date accessed
___Miscellaneous notes

> **Maximize efficiency with a handy checklist**
> A checklist for both on-site and online information-gathering helps make the most of research time.

Online Research

Ensuring Efficiency
___Make a comfortable workspace
___Use a screen you can see easily
___Use a comfortable chair
___Have an adjacent writing space
___Keep contextual materials handy
___Keep food & drink away
___Take breaks to walk & stretch

Advance Tools
___List of repositories & URLs
___List of sources & call numbers
___List of research goals & questions
___Research Log & Documentation Form

Online Information-Gathering
___Print documents if possible
___Make legible notes
___Transcribe notes ASAP

Source Documentation
___Author/creator
___Title
___Type of work
___Publication place & date
___Page number, section, etc.
___Repository location & call number
___URL, date posted, & date accessed
___Miscellaneous notes

Research Execution

Now that you have planned your work, it is time to "work your plan" and actually carry out the research. The three components of research execution are (1) gathering information from the sources you identified, both on-site and online; (2) keeping a research log and documenting sources; and (3) allowing time and space for improvisation and serendipity. At left is a research execution checklist for both on-site and online information gathering.

Gathering Information On-Site & Online

For on-site visits to libraries and archives, your advance planning has prepared you well: You have your librarian/archivist contacts, call numbers for books, records, and microfilm, plenty of note-taking materials, laptop, phone, recording device, and a real camera. When you are on-site in real time at a library or archives, there is also a real-time consideration that is not part of the on-paper plan: Your attitude and behavior. In short, try your utmost to be the happy, trouble-free guest. Be on time for appointments. Follow all the rules-of-the-house. Use pencils, not pens or markers. Handle materials delicately. Turn on whatever charm or personality you may have. And try to restrain yourself from chirping to the research staff about your complete generation-by-generation genealogy all the way back to Fred Flintstone. Your enthusiasm will be welcome, but spare our valued partners from the coma-inducing details. When you are the happy, trouble-free, and grateful guest, librarians and archivists will think well of you and be more willing to go the extra mile for you in the future.

For on-site visits to rural or urban landscapes, buildings, or cemeteries, your plan has prepared you with maps and directions. These on-site visits are no time for research navel-gazing. You have spent your time and gas money to get there, so make sure to keep your eyes and brain open for context. For example, when visiting neighborhoods and landscapes, use your historic maps with your contemporary maps to help understand the changes through time. On cemetery visits, explore not only the gravestone of your subject, but those gravestones around it extending in a healthy radius. Take photos and make accurate notes, because backtracking with on-site information gathering is more time-consuming and expensive than simply revisiting a website.

For the execution of your online information gathering, stick with your organizational plan (research by source category, geography, period, or individual) for maximum time efficiency. As you comb through your selected *sources* for *information* relevant to your research question, you *will* make unexpected discoveries. When you are sitting before your office computer with mountains of source material from around the world just a mouse click away, such discoveries are both a blessing and a curse. Exploring the random discovery immediately will get you off your track and off your plan. But that spur-of-the-moment detour might also yield valuable information and suggest other avenues of inquiry. Experience will be your guide on when to depart from your plan. This is a topic of subsequent discussion in this chapter.

Keeping a Research Log & Documenting Sources

Essential to efficient execution of your research plan – on-site or online – are your *research log* (pg. 29) and *source documentation forms* (pg. 22). The research log, whether in hard-copy or digital form, can be a simple form that includes the following suggested fields: date of search/access; research goal; record name; record type; repository & location; URL or call number; text/image file name (if applicable); and miscellaneous notes, analysis, or transcription. Your research log will help you stay on track with research goals, keep track of URLs and file names, and avoid time-consuming backtracking. In an extended information-rich project, the research log is also an aid in assessing and analyzing the volume of information collected.

For both on-site and online information gathering, meticulously and obsessively record the citation information for each source consulted in your research onto your *source documentation forms*. The forms or database you prepared at the planning stage will help you record the essential citation details for footnotes and bibliographies. Fields on the source documentation form include: the source (book, article, or record); author/creator; publisher, location & date; page numbers; repository location; call number/URL; date accessed; and miscellaneous research notes. The goal, of course, is to ensure that readers of your work in the present or distant future will be able to follow the logic of your narrative and verify your sources.

The Micro-Historian's Guide to
RESEARCH, EVIDENCE, & CONCLUSIONS
Research Execution

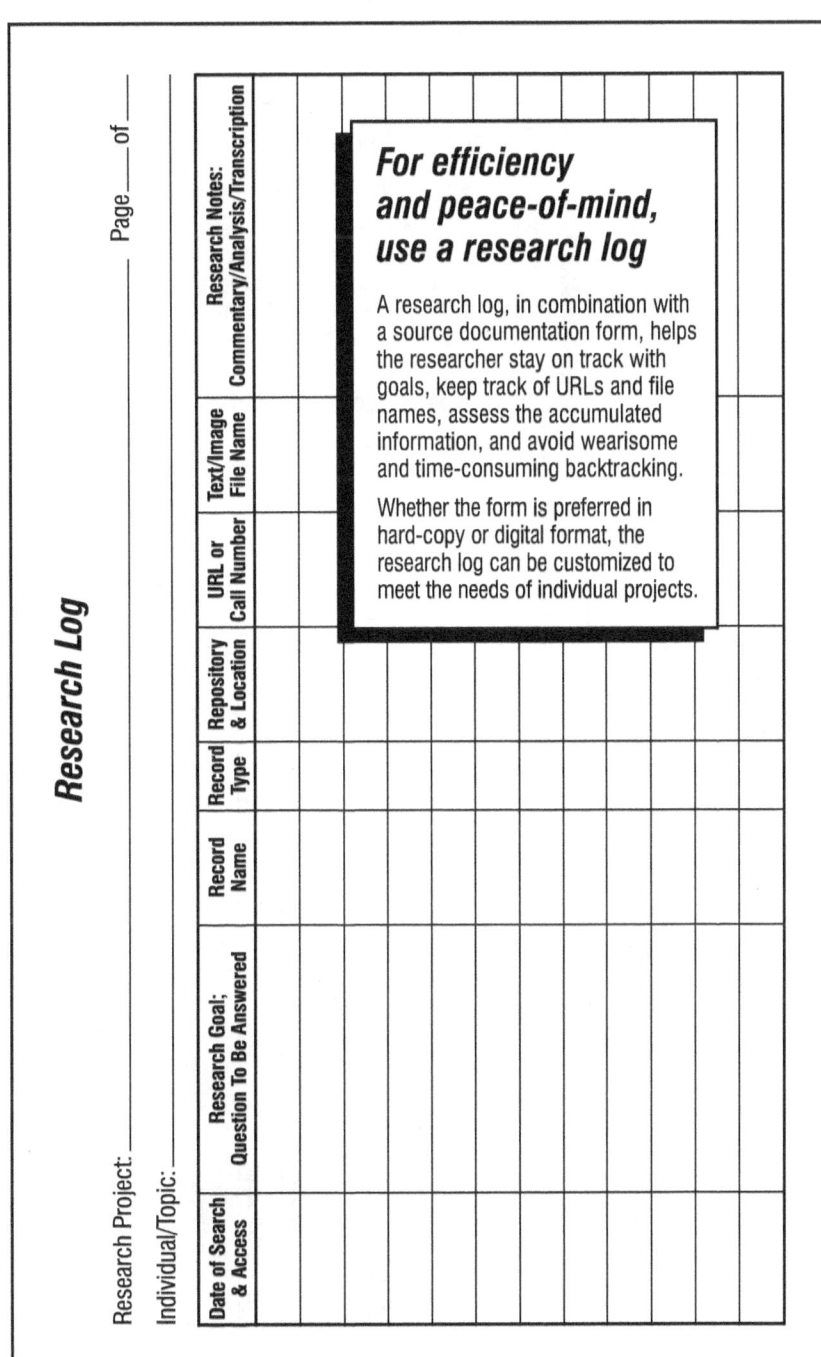

For efficiency and peace-of-mind, use a research log

A research log, in combination with a source documentation form, helps the researcher stay on track with goals, keep track of URLs and file names, assess the accumulated information, and avoid wearisome and time-consuming backtracking.

Whether the form is preferred in hard-copy or digital format, the research log can be customized to meet the needs of individual projects.

The Micro-Historian's Guide to
RESEARCH, EVIDENCE, & CONCLUSIONS
Research Execution

Research Extract Form

Research Project: _____
Individual/Topic: _____
Respository: _____ Call #: _____
Page: ___ of ___

Source Title: _____
Source Description: _____
Indexed: _____ Condition: _____ Date: _____
Time Period / Names & Topics Searched: _____
Search Objective: _____
Research Notes: _____

> ### For fragile sources, use a research extract form
> Primary source documents are often too fragile to permit handling for photocopying, scanning, or photography. Use a research extract form to record information from such delicate documents when working onsite at research repositories.

The Micro-Historian's Guide to
RESEARCH, EVIDENCE, & CONCLUSIONS   *Research Execution*

When consulting sources on-site that cannot be copied or accessed later online, be especially attentive to transcribing narrative passages and direct quotations accurately. For example, for fragile sources for which handling or copying are restricted, use a *research extract form* (pg. 30) with ample room for notes and accurate, legible transcriptions. Keyboard in your transcription from the handwritten form as soon as possible to avoid misreading your own handwriting months later. You don't want to be the one responsible for an error that might be compounded years later on the Internet and spread like a virus.

Regarding the documentation of sources while executing your research: Very handy to have alongside your computer, or to pack on research trips, is *Citing Online Historical Resources Evidence! Style*, a Genealogical Publishing Co. "QuickSheet" based on the books by Elizabeth Shown Mills. The sturdy 11"x17" laminated sheet is folded to letter-size, and is packed with citation examples for almost every conceivable record type a researcher will encounter.[1] The documentation of sources is discussed separately in Appendix III: Source Citation 101, which addresses the slight differences in citation format among three main arbiters, the *Chicago Manual of Style*, the *MLA Style Manual*, and *Evidence Explained*. Whenever you become exasperated by the tedium of source documentation, once again just remember that the reason for doing it in the first place is so that others can verify and fully understand your great work. So whatever citation format you choose (or create!), apply it consistently throughout your project so future scholars can figure it out.

Chicago Manual of Style footnote/endnote citations

Footnote and endnote citations include the author/creator/editor, title, publisher, publication place & date, and details such as series, section, or page numbers. Books and websites are italicized. Article titles are in quotation marks. Publication data is within parentheses. Websites are regarded as the online equivalent of books.

Book: (1) Herkimer Oglethorpe. *My Lazy Life of Sloth, Indolence, and Redundancy.* (King of Prussia, Pa.: Petunia Press, 2014), pg. 577-579.

Article: (2) Hiram Fizzwater, "Fifty Ways to Mow the Front Lawn," *The Artful Yard Man* (Summer 2016): 9-12. (Deep Valley, N.Y.: Deep Publications, 2016).

Website: (3) Mundo Millflap, "Beatnik on the Bongos: Greenwich Village in the 1950s," *CoolCat Magazine* (Fall 2005), accessed June 5, 2018, *https://www.coolcat.hip/Fall05/BeatBongos.html*.

Allowing for Improvisation & Serendipity

In the introduction to *The Micro-Historian's Guide to Research, Evidence, & Conclusions*, one point of emphasis was that the book serve as a guide, not a straitjacket. In this chapter, that means that despite the wisdom of executing research according to a well-thought-out plan, it is important to make allowances – in both time and intellectual space – for improvisation and serendipity.

As in any craft, mastery of the research craft is built on discipline. And as in any craft, the experience gained while acquiring mastery builds confidence in when and how to creatively improvise. In the research craft, this means knowing when to depart from your planned source exploration in order to explore peripheral sources or topics suggested by your research.

Every history or genealogy researcher, novice or pro, has a story of following a hunch or taking a detour down a blind alley, and making an unexpected discovery of surprising relevance to the original research inquiry. For the novice, that kind of discovery is usually the result of many detours down a Manhattan's-worth of blind alleys. With experience, however, the focused researcher becomes more selective about which peripheral sources and topics to explore. Discoveries that have propelled research to new heights, or that have inspired new research inquiries, are often described as "lucky." But with applied experience, judgment, resourcefulness, and industriousness, you can improve your "blind alley selection," and as in other areas of life, you can "make your own luck."

History methodology scholar John Tosh addressed this topic in *The Pursuit of History: Aims, Methods, and New Directions in the Study of History* (6th ed., 2015). The question facing the researcher is whether to follow the inquiry-based research plan, or whether to allow the content of the source to direct the inquiry. Tosh's view is that while the problem-oriented approach seems obvious, it can be difficult to determine ahead of time what sources are the most relevant. Sometimes it is the improbable sources discovered along the way that turn out to be the most revealing. By directing attention only to the obvious sources, the historian might be drawn into the bias of a particular source's creator. The too-narrow focus on pre-selected sources may lead to a context-drained misinterpretation.[2]

Historians commonly re-route research inquiries based upon new findings within selected sources ... or the discovery of previously unknown sources. The historian should be flexible enough to modify a research inquiry based on new questions arising from the sources, in order to tap the sources' full potential.[3]

So how do you decide when to research down a blind alley? Ask yourself if the payoff will be worth the time and effort. Ask yourself if the blind alley excursion is relevant to your research inquiry. Or are you just following your curiosity because it's fun diversion? (This is OK! Fun is good! Essential even. But it is not necessarily part of your research project.) Ask yourself what is the probability or possibility of discovering something meaningful that addresses your research inquiry. Unfortunately there is no shortcut to the experience needed to answer some of these questions. As John Tosh wrote: "The true master of the craft is someone whose sense of what questions can profitably be asked has been sharpened by a lifetime's exposure to the sources in all their variety."[4]

So explore your sources according to plan, but be open to all the new questions that arise. Budget some time and brain-space for peripheral explorations. You might even make a serendipitous discovery that leads to a new research inquiry. You might have to make a new plan. And then the fun begins again.

A quipster acquaintance once said, when comparing planning to luck, that "Sometimes, when planning don't work, serendipity do."

Some practical examples of information gathering:

• The execution of information gathering for *Chauncey Richmond & "The Old Buckbee": The Story of a Banjo, Its Maker, and Its Player* (2018)[5] proceeded according to plan. The exploration of newspaper articles and banjo catalogs of the late 19th century, however, suggested a new avenue of inquiry about the relationship between the Bronx, N.Y. banjo-manufacturing Buckbee families [J. H. Buckbee I (1837-1890) and J. H. Buckbee II (1867-1942)] and the family of Robert I. Lomas, Jr. (1850-1927). Because of the uncertainty of meaningful research findings, this inquiry was saved for last, and it did involve some backtracking to census sources, and deeper dives into records of real estate transactions. But ultimately the information derived from this new inquiry proved essential to the Buckbee banjo factory narrative. William B. Lomas (1859-1941), known professionally as "Will Lyle," was a banjo entertainer of note in New York, whose "Lomas Patent Banjo" was manufactured by J. H. Buckbee in the late 1880s. The brother of "Will Lyle" was Robert I. Lomas, Jr., who was also the father of Marion Ward Lomas, who married George E. Buckbee, the second son of J. H. Buckbee I, in

The Micro-Historian's Guide to
RESEARCH, EVIDENCE, & CONCLUSIONS　　　　　*Research Execution*

1893. Robert I. Lomas, Jr. was a co-investor in the extended family's real estate dealings after the banjo factory assets were liquidated in 1897. In 1900 he was a major player in the development of the former banjo factory site into a row of four large apartment buildings in the fast-growing Tremont section of the Bronx, N.Y. Therefore the detour off the research track proved fruitful, revealing a possible motive for the liquidation of Buckbee banjo factory assets.

• The execution of information gathering for *Cigar Box Manipulation & Balance* (1983)[6] proceeded according to plan. The main content of the book was the technique of this physically-demanding object-manipulation specialty, but a brief section on its history was essential. The realm of juggling and acrobatics is not quite as well-documented as the history of kings, generals, and wars, so for the most part, its relatively few history sources are from the last 400 years. Fortunately, thanks to the popularity of Indian, Chinese, and Japanese juggling artists in late-19th-century European music halls, newspaper and magazine coverage was plentiful, and included not only lengthy reviews, but also interviews with the performers, who were regarded as novelties from exotic lands. For the history of box manipulation, an indispensable source was an article by Japanese juggler M. Gintaro [(Gintaro Mizuhara (1875-1952)], translated by Wellesley Pain, in London's *Strand Magazine* of December 1914, entitled "Japanese Juggling Tricks and How They Were Invented."[7] Gintaro related the story of a 17th-century Japanese prisoner, who despite being fed meager prison rations, kept gaining more muscle and getting more fit. Apparently the prisoner was using wood blocks, supplied to inmates as pillows to elevate and protect their long hair, for exercise, manipulating them in all sorts of creative ways. When the prisoner demonstrated his skills for the guards, he was taken to the warden, who was so impressed that he had the prisoner perform for the civil authorities. Eventually the prisoner was released to become an appointed court entertainer. Excerpts from the magazine article were included in the book, even though the box-juggling origin story was unverifiable.

But research never ceases. Several decades after publication of the book, a research colleague in Europe discovered more to the story in a new source of private letters. It is possible that M. Gintaro fashioned his uplifting tale of the prisoner as a safe diversion from a different box-juggling origin story. Apparently the manipulation and balancing of towers of "pillow blocks" in Japan centuries ago was known to be a type of preliminary entertainment provided by male prostitutes for their customers. If this origin story was known during original research for the book, would I have gone down the "blind alley" in pursuit of an equally unverifiable story? Or would I have been satisfied with the magazine article at its face-value? Alas, the historian always wants to know more. Who knows what may be down the blind alley?

• Information gathering for *The HABS and the HABs NOTs: Documenting the Architecture of Newburyport in the Historic American Buildings Survey* (2017)[8] proceeded according to plan. Among the federal HABS projects was documentation of buildings in Newburyport, Mass. that were slated for demolition in 1934 to make way for a highway. The information-rich sources of HABS documentation held by the U.S. Library of Congress might convince some that no more research was needed. My microhistory focus, however, prompted me to seek information about property owners, displaced residents, and salvaged houses. By reading miles of newspaper microfilm, I learned that most of the houses were rented (many by non-English-speakers), and owned by absentee landlords glad to sell out. Newspaper reports indicated that the few public hearings on the project were attended only by businessmen and politicians. But one report about the recently-deposed "bad boy mayor," Andrew J. "Bossy" Gillis (1896-1965), made a "blind alley" diversion and new inquiry imperative. In this instance, the findings were uproarious. He wanted the highway construction re-routed through his property instead – an old jail where he was once an inmate – because he was having trouble selling it. His plan was tossed. Years later, *Time* magazine reported: "Bossy Gillis still looks as seedy as Burpee's spring catalog."[9]

NOTES to Research Execution
(1) Elizabeth Shown Mills. *QuickSheet - Citing Online Historical Resources - Evidence! Style.* (Baltimore, Md.: Genealogical Publishing Co., 2007).
(2) John Tosh. *The Pursuit of History: Aims, Methods, and New Directions in the Study of History* (6th ed.). (New York, N.Y.: Routledge, 2015), pg. 99-100.
(3) Ibid., pg. 100.
(4) Ibid., pg. 100.
(5) R. W. Bacon. *Chauncey Richmond and "The Old Buckbee": The Story of a Banjo, Its Maker, and Its Player.* (Newburyport, Mass.: Variety Arts Press, 2018).
(6) R. W. Bacon. *The Juggler's Manual of Cigar Box Manipulation & Balance.* (Groveland, Mass.: Variety Arts Press, 1983).
(7) M. Gintaro. "Japanese Juggling Tricks and How They Were Invented," *Strand Magazine* (December 1914). (London, England: Strand Publishing Co., 1914).
(8) R. W. Bacon. *The HABS and the HABs NOTs: Documenting the Architecture of Newburyport in the Historic American Buildings Survey.* (Newburyport, Mass.: Variety Arts Press, 2017).
(9) "Massachusetts: The Old Zamg." *Time* magazine, December 19, 1949. (New York, N.Y.: Time, Inc., 1949).

Concepts in the Evaluation of Evidence

Evidence defined: *Evidence* is what results from the analysis and interpretation of *information* derived from *sources*.

Evaluation of Evidence for Substance
- Substance (i.e. assess the pieces of information within a record)
- Is it Original/Primary Evidence? (i.e. from the event's time & place)
- Is it Derivative/Secondary Evidence? (i.e. not from the time & place)
- Is it Direct Evidence? (i.e. it answers a question on its own)
- Is it Indirect Evidence? (i.e. it needs corroboration by other evidence)

Evaluation of Evidence for Relevance
- Relevance (i.e. assess degree of usefulness in addressing inquiry)

Evaluation of Evidence for Reliability
- Reliability (i.e. assess conditions & intentions for degree of reliability)
    - Evaluate the originality, genesis, purpose, & authority
    - Evaluate the context of the time & place
    - Evaluate the competence & motive of the creator
- Credibility (i.e. assess thoroughness & logical construct)
    - Primary sources (original records have the highest credibility)
    - Secondary sources (assess the quality of the documentation)

Deriving Facts from Evidence
- Synthesize aggregated analyzed evidence that supports a conclusion
- How? Use your reasoning powers born of knowledge & experience!

Proof Standards & Proof Levels
- Proof (i.e. a conclusion based on an assembled rationale of facts)
- Proof Standards
    - Legal/Deductive Model (deductive evaluation of evidence)
    - Historical/Diplomatics Model (reliability; relational/causal factors)
    - Scientific Method (hypothesis, test, observe, measure, repeat)
    - BCG Genealogical Proof Standard (for "genealogical definition")
- Proof Levels (Assign proof level qualifiers to inconclusive findings.)
    - Certainly
    - Likely
    - Possibly
    - May have
    - Probably
    - Apparently
    - Plausibly
    - Might have

Evaluation of Evidence

Now that the five steps of research are complete – the formulation of the inquiry, the acquisition of context, the survey of sources, the plan for exploring sources, and the information-gathering itself – the time has come for the evaluation of evidence. Within the *information* extracted from the broad selection of *sources* is the *evidence* that the historian or genealogist hopes will satisfy the research inquiry. Ultimately that accumulated evidence may prove a theory, build an argument, or drive a narrative. But what is evidence? And how do historians and genealogists evaluate its relative weight and worth?

Evidence defined. *Evidence* is what results from the analysis and interpretation of *information* derived from *sources*. The two types of evidence are *direct evidence*, which can appear to answer a research question straightaway as a *fact*, and *indirect evidence*, which must be supported by other *information* to reach the level of *fact*. It is important to note that *information* is by itself neutral – only when used to support a particular assertion does it become *evidence*. *Facts* are derived from analyzed *evidence*, and can lead to a *proof*, but evidence itself is not *proof*.[1,2,3,4]

Evaluation for Substance, Relevance, & Reliability

In the preliminary survey of *sources*, the relevant *sources* should be evaluated for *reliability, conditions, and intentions*, although such evaluation may be difficult until probing deeper into each *source*. After *information* is extracted from *sources*, evaluation of *evidence* includes the judgment of whether the *evidence* is *original/primary*, or *derivative/secondary*; whether it is *direct* or *indirect*; and its *substance, relevance, reliability, and credibility*. Repeating some concepts that also pertain to *sources*, these terms are clarified here.

- **Original/primary evidence.** A statement or record made by a witness to or principal of an event, at the time of the event or subsequent to it.[5] Example: A marriage record signed by the minister who performed the ceremony.

The Micro-Historian's Guide to
RESEARCH, EVIDENCE, & CONCLUSIONS   *Evaluation of Evidence*

- **Derivative/secondary evidence.** A statement or record made by an individual who was not a physically present witness to a particular event.[6] Example: Transcripts, databases, your imaginative Aunt Tillie's story about your ancestor crossing the Delaware with George Washington, etc.

- **Direct evidence.** As stated above, information that answers a question on its own, needing no corroboration.[7] Example: A primary source land record or will signed at the date of creation by the subject individual.

- **Indirect evidence.** As stated above, information that contributes to answering a research question, but needs corroborating information to support it.[8] Example: A census record that indicates that a couple is married ... which ideally needs the corroboration of the original primary source marriage record.

- **Substance.** The individual pieces of information within any given record.[9] Example: The multitude of information within one military record, like height, weight, hair color, occupation, and hometown.

- **Relevance.** The degree of usefulness that certain information has in answering a research question.[10] Example: In the research process there is usually considerable information amassed that is of undeniable topical interest, but its degree of relevance may be unknown until the analysis of all related information.

- **Reliability.** The preliminary survey evaluated sources for reliability. The same considerations are used to evaluate the information for evidence: Originality, genesis, purpose, and authority of the information; the context of its time and place; and the competence and motive of its creator.[11] Example: The "facts" cited in a campaigning politician's tirade are especially low on the reliability-of-evidence scale. (Yet hypothetically, for research on the particular political campaign, the tirade itself would be regarded as primary source direct evidence.)

- **Credibility.** The original record information from a primary source has the highest credibility. The credibility of secondary derivative information found in later published material should be evaluated based on the thoroughness of its documentation and the logical construct of its statements.[12] Example: A smitten and verbose jazz fan's unpublished stream-of-consciousness reviews of Thelonious Monk recordings, scattered with third-hand biographical details picked up from CD inserts, may make good reading and be chock-full of insights, but they will be no match in the credibility department to *Thelonious Monk: The Life and Times of an American Original* (2009)[13] by Robin D. G. Kelly, a magisterial 588-page biography with 99 pages devoted to its 2,802 endnotes.

In evaluating aggregated evidence on a particular issue, one must consider (1) the degree of truth supported by evidence, as the "truth" may be shaped by social, economic, political, or cultural forces; (2) the amount of evidence, as the abundance of evidence in more recent times may not compare with the sparse historical record of an earlier age; and (3) the observer's distance from events, as the perception of an event is influenced by the distance from it.[14]

Deriving Facts from Evidence

Facts. In the ideal hypothetical research project, after the evaluation and analysis of all manner of information – original, derivative, direct, indirect – of different levels of substance, relevance, reliability, and credibility – the researcher/historian/genealogist will use reasoning powers born of knowledge and experience to synthesize individual pieces of supportive evidence into facts.[15] Example: An easy-to-understand example is the one fact of an individual's birth date that is arrived at by analyzing multiple pieces of evidence – census records, church baptismal records, school records, marriage records, military records, and unsourced family genealogy records – no single one of which is authoritative by itself like a birth certificate. But if all the aggregated evidence points to a single birth date, or even birth month, the genealogist can safely assign the fact an "almost certain" proof level.[16]

Understanding Proof Standards & Proof Levels

Proof. In historical and genealogical research, a proof is a conclusion based on an assembled rationale of facts, sometimes referred to as a proof argument. The proof of each individual assertion is based on the rigorous analysis of the totality of relevant, reliable, well-documented, and correlated evidence.[17] (It is important to note that today, in genealogy research, *absolute* or *conclusive proof* of an asserted relationship is possible only through DNA analysis. Before advances in DNA analysis, an astute but tight-lipped professional colleague tersely expressed his jaundiced opinion of genealogy thusly: "Nobody really knows what goes on between the sheets.")

Proof Standards. Professionals in different categories of research – legal, historical, cultural, literary, or scientific – strive in their work to meet a proof standard most appropriate to their specialty. The three most common proof standards are the legal/deductive model, the historical/diplomatics model, and the scientific method. A more rigorous hybrid for genealogy research is the codified Genealogical Proof Standard developed by the Board for Certification of Genealogists (BCG). The following paragraphs explain the four standards:

• **The Legal/Deductive Model.** Most common to the layman is the legal model that calls for deductive evaluation of evidence that either (1) proves a case "beyond a reasonable doubt" (as in criminal cases); (2) proves a case by "clear and convincing evidence" (as in some "life-and-liberty" civil cases); or (3) proves a case by "a preponderance of evidence" (as in civil cases in which conclusions be "more probable than not").[17] Genealogists have moved away from the "preponderance of evidence" terminology in favor of a higher standard.[18]

• **The Historical/Diplomatics Model.** In 1681, Dom Jean Mabillon (1632-1707), a French Maurist monk and history scholar, published *De re diplomatica*, a study of editing, handwriting, document structure, and the importance of distinguishing original sources from forgeries. In discussion of his rationale, Mabillon wrote in 1681:"I do not deny that in fact some documents are false and others interpolated, but all of them should not be dismissed for that reason. Rather, it is necessary to devise and hand down rules for distinguishing genuine manuscripts from those that are false and interpolated. ... I undertook this task after long familiarity and daily experience with these documents. For almost twenty years I had devoted my studies and energies to reading and examining ancient manuscripts and archives, and the published collections of ancient documents. ... I compared and weighed them with one another that I might be able to compile a body of knowledge which was not merely scanty and meager, but as accurate and as well-tested as possible in a field which had not been previously investigated."[19] Today, *diplomatics* is the term for the study of the properties of charters and official documents to ascertain their authenticity. The fields of history and genealogy have borrowed principles of diplomatics in the study of the physical form of a document, its layout, date, seals, and handwriting – as well as its language, vocabulary, tradition, genesis, originality, authenticity, creator, motive, and meaning – to evaluate evidence for substance, relevance, reliability, and credibility. The historical/diplomatics model also considers the relationship of historical events, and possible causal factors (social, cultural, economic, biological, racial, technological, political, geographical, and environmental) within the particular period of study.[20]

- **The Scientific Method.** In the scientific method, most applicable to research in the physical sciences, a hypothesis is formulated, then tested for its validity in controlled experiments that produce measurable results. The measured results from repeated experiments are compared with predictions in the hypothesis. Comparison and observation may lead to a new hypothesis, and the cycle of experimentation, measurement, and observation begins again.[21] The values of discipline, consistency, and objectivity that define the scientific method are embraced by researchers and scholars in all fields, and the values are as unassailable as motherhood and apple pie. But for history researchers exploring the past, while predictive experiments about the future may not be part of the toolkit, for the genealogist researching individual relationships in a narrowly-focused time and place, the repeated hypothesis-and-test approach can be useful.

- **The BCG Genealogical Proof Standard.** Developed by the Board for Certification of Genealogists (BCG) in 2000 and revised in 2014, the Genealogical Proof Standard has five components: "(1) Reasonably exhaustive research, (2) Complete and accurate source citations, (3) Thorough analysis and correlation, (4) Resolution of conflicting evidence, and (5) Soundly written conclusion based on the strongest evidence."[22] Explanatory text amplifies each component. This proof standard sets the bar high for the "genealogical definition" of individuals, and is enthusiastically embraced by professional genealogists, but it is not always applicable to the work of the historian.

What?! Your research will not tie up with a tidy bow?!

What if you work through your sources, extract information, evaluate your evidence, gather your facts, and work through a proof standard – and after all that, you determine that your research inquiry is not definitively answered ... and that there are still loose ends and unanswered questions?

Sorry, but in history and genealogy research, there is never any guarantee that you will answer every question about a person's life and times, prove every relationship, or solve every puzzle. One reason is that the questions we pose about the past today or in the future might never have occurred to the people of a different time and place. Therefore, in a given historical period, there may be no formal record or informal narrative to serve as evidence to answer our 21st-century research inquiry. So the unanswered questions remain open for the next round of research ... or the fresh energy of the next researcher. Meanwhile, what you are unable to find out in your research – and why – can be just as illuminating as what you do find.

Proof levels. Fortunately, historians and genealogists have learned that assigning proof levels to inconclusive findings, based on thorough analysis of their evidence, mitigates the frustration or despair of unanswered research questions. A proof level is determined by the researcher from their objective reading of the "sliding scale of relative confidence" for each assertion. In a detailed summary of research or a flowing narrative history, the proof level is expressed by qualifiers like plausibly, possibly, likely, probably, and certainly. The meanings of these qualifiers, of course, are not precisely fixed, and are subjective to both the writer and reader. Although individual history and genealogy authors may use proof level qualifiers differently, the ideal is consistency throughout a summary or narrative, so that readers become familiar with the researcher's own "sliding scale" and terminology.[23]

The following are some commonly-used qualifiers in history and genealogy writing, with dictionary definitions from *Merriam-Webster's Collegiate Dictionary* (11th ed., 2009) and proof level definitions gathered from across the genealogy field[24]:

- **Certainly.** Dictionary: "Known or proved to be true. Indisputable." Genealogical meaning: No reasonable doubt.

- **Probably.** Dictionary: "Supported by evidence strong enough to establish presumption, but not proof. Without much doubt." Genealogical meaning: Clearly more than 50% likelihood.

- **Likely.** Dictionary: "Having a high probability of being true." Genealogical meaning: Slightly more than 50% likelihood.

- **Apparently.** Dictionary: "Clear or manifest to the understanding. Appearing as actual to the eye or mind." Genealogical meaning: A presumption of likelihood.

- **Possibly.** Dictionary: "Being something that may or may not be true or actual." Genealogical meaning: Some supporting evidence, but not proven. Less than 50% likelihood.

- **Plausibly.** Dictionary: "Appearing worthy of belief." Genealogical meaning: Within the realm of possibility, but with no evidence.

Other useful qualifying phrases will suggest themselves in the narrative crafting process, like "may have," "could have," and "might have." But most qualifiers will be permutations of the "possibly, probably, certainly" family of adverbs. As we move closer to the "Conclusions" section on writing the research summary, it is important to note that proof level qualifiers should be used in the right place in a sentence to avoid ambiguity. Consider this sentence: "Joe Schmoe, born in 1854, probably joined the circus in Hay Springs, Nebraska in 1886." Did he just "probably" join the circus? Or did he really join the circus, "probably in 1886"?

When one has research complete to a satisfactory point, and the accumulated evidence, source citations, facts, proofs, non-proofs, plus command of the vocabulary of qualifiers, one then has the raw material at hand to move on to writing the narrative summary of conclusions.

Some practical examples of evidence evaluation:

• Key *sources* explored in the research of John Henry Buckbee's banjo and drum factory for *Chauncey Richmond & "The Old Buckbee": The Story of a Banjo, Its Maker, and Its Player* (2018)[25] were maps and city directories of the time (1860s-1910s), and more recently published local histories. The maps and city directories were *primary sources* because they were created by individuals of the time and place. The *information* extracted from the maps and directories was *direct*, even though errors may have cropped up along the print production process. The published local history, *The Birth of the Bronx 1609-1900*, by Lloyd Ultan and Gary Hermalyn (2000)[??], was a *secondary derivative source* containing direct information about the chronology of jurisdictional and civil boundary changes in what is now the Bronx, N.Y. All of the *information* selectively extracted from the maps, directories, and published local history was regarded as *evidence*, because all the interrelated geographic information addressed the *research inquiry* – the establishment and evolution of John Henry Buckbee's banjo factory. In evaluating the *evidence* for *relevance*, most *relevant* were the 19th-century maps showing the location of the Osborn & Buckbee Drum Factory before all the street names were changed in the Tremont neighborhood of the Bronx. Least *relevant* was information from the late 19th-century city directories after the street names had stabilized. In evaluating the *evidence* for *reliability*, the fine detail of the New York City fire insurance maps suggested high *reliability*, while the New York city directories, massive compilation projects fraught with the possibility of typesetting errors, scored lower on the *reliability* scale. The *facts* drawn from analysis of this particular geographic and civil boundary *evidence* did not directly address the *research inquiry* about the reticent John Henry Buckbee. But correlated together, the multiple *facts* did synthesize into a *proof* that the factory was located on the same block in Tremont for all but the very end of its business life span. The business did not hop around New York as some previous researchers have interpreted based only on the different addresses in the city directories through the years. As with the research into Chauncey Richmond as a vaudeville impresario, this *research inquiry* to find out about the man behind the bustling Bronx banjo factory also required no specific *proof* in any aspect. Although much *evidence* was gathered about the banjo factory and its business history, very little *information* illuminated the elder John Henry Buckbee himself. Therefore the *historical/diplomatic* approach to *conclusions* called for, at times, generous use of *proof level qualifiers* such as *"likely"* and *"may have"* when stymied by the absence of *proof*-worthy *facts*.

• Key *sources* explored for *A Micro-History of the Tannersville Four-Corners* (2011)[26], a 19th-to-20th-century local history of the bustling crossroads of a mountain town in the northern High Peaks region of New York's Catskill Mountains, included maps, photographs, census records, newspapers, business directories, published local histories, family genealogies, and personal interviews. The maps, photographs, census records, newspapers, and business directories were *primary sources,* i.e. created by individuals of the time and place. The *information* extracted was *direct*, even though newspaper reporters and census enumerators have never been infallible. The published local history compilations and family genealogies were *secondary derivative sources*. The interviews with longtime residents, one a revered nonagenarian local historian, were both *primary* and *secondary sources*. When interviewees spoke of their own first-person recollections, the interview was a *primary source* for the specific topic. When interviewees spoke of their interpretation of earlier local history of which they were not a witness, the interview was a *secondary derivative source*. All the *information* selectively extracted from the above *sources* was regarded as *evidence* relating to the *research inquiry* that sought understanding of the town's evolution "from a 'tavern at the crossroads' serving seasonal 'bark-peelers' of the early 19th century, to its late-19th-century 'grand hotel' era as a summer destination for sweltering New Yorkers." In evaluating the *evidence* for *relevance*, the most *relevant* were the maps indicating property owners and businesses, and the corroborating census records. The least *relevant* were some family genealogies that concentrated on geographically-distant family lines. In evaluating the *evidence* for *reliability*, the detailed 20th-century Sanborn fire insurance maps of the town were the most *reliable*. Least *reliable* were the family genealogies compromised by distracting, unsubstantiated content taking the family back to the Norman Conquest ... or Charlemagne. The *facts* drawn from *evidence* indicated that through the years, the ebb-and-flow of social (immigration, population growth), economic (Depression years), technological (steamboat, rail, auto transportation), and cultural forces (ethnic family norms) brought a succession of different ethnic groups – New England Yankee, Irish, German, Jewish, Syrian, and Armenian – to own and operate – and then sell out – the businesses and hotels clustered around the Tannersville Four Corners. As for a *proof* derived from discovered *facts*, in the realm of *microhistory*, the *research inquiry* does not necessarily lead to, nor require, a *proof*. In fact, the goal in this *research inquiry* was rather an illumination of understanding, not a proof of some advanced thesis.

- The key *source* explored in the research of the decrepit no-name banjo that beget the book, *Chauncey Richmond & "The Old Buckbee": The Story of a Banjo, Its Maker, and Its Player* (2018)[27] was the material object itself. The banjo in its unrestored state, with its lone "Tremont No. 98" marking on the dowel stick, was a *primary source*. Other *primary sources* from the time and place were the Charles Bruno & Son musical instrument catalogs (1886-1890) and the late-19th-century maps showing the Buckbee banjo factory in the Tremont section of the Bronx. N.Y. An important *secondary source* was the masterful book, *America's Instrument: The Banjo in the 19th Century*, by Philip F. Gura and James F. Bollman (1999)[28], which included documentation of J. H. Buckbee being a "ghost" manufacturer for wholesalers like Charles Bruno & Son. The *information* from the banjo, the instrument catalogs, and the maps was *direct information*, while the *information* from *America's Instrument* was *indirect*, or *derivative*. All of the *information* selectively extracted from the maps and instrument catalogs, and from "reading" the banjo, was regarded as *evidence* because all the interrelated *information* addressed the *research inquiry* – the "who, what, when, where, and why" of its manufacture. In evaluating the *evidence*, of equal *relevance* were the "Tremont" inscription on the banjo dowel stick, and the maps showing the Buckbee banjo factory in Tremont, Bronx. N.Y. For positive identification of the banjo, the detailed drawing and descriptions of the "Model #102" in the Charles Bruno & Son musical instrument catalog were essential *evidence*. All *evidence* from the maps, catalogs, and banjo was deemed to have high *substance* and *reliability*. Correlated together, the multiple *facts* derived from the *evidence* did synthesize into a *proof* that the "Tremont No. 98" banjo was a J. H. Buckbee "no-name" instrument made prior to the circulation of the 1886-1890 George Bruno & Son wholesale catalog, which featured the virtually identical "Model #102." The *level of confidence* assigned to this *proof* ascended only to *"likely,"* however – a more than 50% likelihood of being true, but just short of *"probably."* *"Certainly"* would have required the *source* and *evidence* of an earlier original catalog with the "No. 98" banjo and an accompanying picture, as it is quite possible that Buckbee's model numbers, so rarely found in the first place, were not assigned in chronological order. Therefore this caveat repeats: Once again the *historical/diplomatic* approach to *conclusions* called for, at times, generous use of *proof level qualifiers* such as *"likely"* and *"may have"* when stymied by the absence of *proof*-worthy *facts*.

NOTES to Evaluation of Evidence

(1) Donn Devine, "Evidence Analysis," in *Professional Genealogy: A Manual for Researchers, Writers, Editors, Lecturers, and Librarians.* (Elizabeth Shown Mills, ed.). (Baltimore, Md.: Genealogical Publishing Co., 2001), pg. 329-331.

(2) Val D. Greenwood *The Researcher's Guide to American Genealogy (4th Ed.).* (Baltimore, Md.: Genealogical Publishing Co., 2017), pg. 80-82.

(3) Wayne C. Booth; Gregory G. Colomb; & Joseph M. Williams. *The Craft of Research.* (Chicago, Ill.: University of Chicago Press, 2008), pg. 138-150.

(4) Elizabeth Shown Mills. *Evidence Explained: Citing History Sources from Artifacts to Cyberspace* (3rd ed.). (Baltimore, Md.: Genealogical Publishing Co., 2017), pg. 22-26.

(5) Mills, *Evidence Explained*, pg. 22; Greenwood, pg. 87; Booth, Colomb, & Williams, pg. 76.

(6) Mills, *Evidence Explained*, pg. 24-25; Devine, pg. 334; Greenwood, pg. 87; Booth, Colomb, & Williams, pg. 76.

(7) Mills, *Evidence Explained*, pg. 25; Devine, pg. 334; Greenwood, pg. 87; Booth, Colomb, & Williams, pg. 142-144.

(8) Mills, *Evidence Explained*, pg. 25; Devine, pg. 334; Greenwood, pg. 87; Booth, Colomb, & Williams, pg. 142-144.

(9) Robert Charles Anderson. *Elements of Genealogical Analysis.* (Boston, Mass.: New England Historic Genealogical Society, 2014), pg. 2, 133.

(10) Devine, pg. 335; Booth, Colomb, & Williams, pg. 149-150.

(11) Mills, *Evidence Explained*, pg. 33; Devine, pg. 337; Anderson, pg. 2-3, 132.

(12) Devine, pg. 335.

(13) Robin D. G. Kelly. *Thelonious Monk: The Life and Times of an American Original.* (New York, N.Y.: Free Press/Simon & Schuster, 2009).

(14) Devine, pg. 337; John Tosh. *The Pursuit of History: Aims, Methods, and New Directions in the Study of History* (6th ed.). (New York, N.Y.: Routledge, 2015), pg. 106-107.

(15) Mills, *Evidence Explained*, pg. 18; Anderson, pg. 83; Booth, Colomb, & Williams, pg. 39.

(16) Devine, pg. 340; Greenwood, pg. 82-83.

(17) Mills, *Evidence Explained*, pg. 26; Devine, pg. 338; Greenwood, pg. 81-85; Anderson, pg. 83, 106.

(18) Devine, pg. 330-331, 338-340; Greenwood, pg. 82-83.

(19) Jean Mabillon. *De re diplomatica* (1681). Translated by Richard Wertis as *On Diplomatics*, in *Historians at Work - Vol. II.* (New York, N.Y.: Harper & Row, 1972), pg. 165.

(20) John Tosh. *The Pursuit of History: Aims, Methods, and New Directions in the Study of History* (6th ed.). (New York, N.Y.: Routledge, 2015), pg. 103; Martha Howell & John Prevenier. *From Reliable Sources: An Introduction to Historical Methods.* (Ithaca, N.Y.: Cornell University Press, 2001), pg. 8, 41, 100.

(21) Devine, pg. 338-339.

(22) The Board for Certification of Genealogists. *Genealogy Standards.* (Orem, Utah: Ancestry Publishing, 2014).

(23) Mills, *Evidence Explained*, pg. 19-20; Booth, Colomb, & Williams, pg. 218; Christine Rose, "Family Histories," in *Professional Genealogy: A Manual for Researchers, Writers, Editors, Lecturers, and Librarians.* (Elizabeth Shown Mills, ed.). (Baltimore, Md.: Genealogical Publishing Co., 2001), pg. 462-463.

(24) Mills, *Evidence Explained*, pg. 19-20.

(25) R. W. Bacon. *Chauncey Richmond and "The Old Buckbee": The Story of a Banjo, Its Maker, and Its Player.* (Newburyport, Mass.: Variety Arts Press, 2018).

(26) R. W. Bacon. *A Micro-History of the Tannersville Four-Corners.* ((Newburyport, Mass.: Variety Arts Press, 2008, 2011).

(27) Bacon, *Chauncey Richmond and "The Old Buckbee": The Story of a Banjo, Its Maker, and Its Player.*

(28) Philip F. Gura & James F. Bollman. *America's Instrument: The Banjo in the Nineteenth Century.* (Chapel Hill, N.C.: University of North Carolina Press, 1999).

Principles of 21st-Century Microhistory

Microhistory defined:
Microhistory is a subset of social history that reduces the scale of observation in the study of events, actions, locales, individuals, or small social units. Emphasis has been on the under-recorded history of "ordinary lives" and "outliers," but more recently the approach has been applied to social, economic, technological, and cultural topics.

Groundbreaking microhistory theoreticians & authors:
- Carlo Ginzburg (b. 1939)
- Giovanni Levi (b. 1939)
- Alf Ludtke (b. 1943)
- Sigurdur G. Magnusson (b. 1957)
- George R. Stewart (1895-1980)
- Laurel Thatcher Ulrich (b. 1938)
- Mark Kurlansky (b. 1948)
- Alan Taylor (b. 1955)

Microhistory principles & characteristics:

- Microhistory studies employ a reduced scale of observation.
- Microhistory studies focus on an individual, small social unit, or locale.
- Microhistory studies focus on daily life instead of monumental events.
- Microhistory studies focus on ordinary lives, or even "outliers," instead of the privileged ruling class.
- Microhistory studies may focus on a single sociological, economic, technological, or cultural topic.
- Microhistory narratives infuse the human scale of ordinary everyday life into larger historical abstractions.
- Microhistory narratives may incorporate the author's methodology and research process.
- Microhistory narratives may include commentary that notes the gaps in knowledge or documentation.
- Microhistory narratives may include conclusions and analysis … or be inconclusive and observational/descriptive only.
- Microhistory studies may … or may not … link the particular micro observations to the universal macro history of the time and place.

Formulation of Conclusions

Did somebody say "conclusion"? In history or genealogy research, are we ever truly finished? In the research context, this loaded word needs clarification.

When a research project reaches the point of "conclusion," the work of messy history and pure genealogy diverge. In some ways, genealogists, even though working to a high proof standard, have it easier than historians. The goal of the genealogist is the clear-cut proof of a relationship, so that an individual is "genealogically defined." An individual is said to be "genealogically defined" when there is at least one piece of evidence about each parent, one piece of evidence for each spouse, and one piece of evidence for each child.[1] The genealogist's aggregated evidence may point to a conclusive "yes" or "no" answer about a particular relationship, or may lead to the assignment of a proof-level qualifier like "probably" or "possibly."

The job of the historian, on the other hand, is not only the facile presentation of aggregated evidence, but an interpretation that derives meaning from the evidence. Yet the history researcher's wide-ranging and messy evidence of chaotic human affairs may never yield a conclusive "yes" or "no" answer about anything.

The individual researcher's particular philosophy of history will determine the interpretation. Historians, even those with the ultimate in credentials and reputation, come in many flavors. There are the majority of historians who worship dispassionate objectivity. There are popular author-historians who are great literary storytellers. There are historians who deliberately ignore certain context to advance a particular social or political argument. There are historians for whom comprehensive context is everything. There are broad-view social historians who aim to synthesize massive amounts of data. And there are microhistorians who reduce the scale of observation to reveal the detail of individual lives or small social groups. There are historians who mix-and-match approaches depending on the topic. For every approach, and perhaps for every historian, the idea of what constitutes a "conclusion" will be different.

Objectivity in Conclusions ... and Limits of Knowledge

Here is a question for you: What is your favorite and most foundational work of history writing? One that has informed your world view? One that, in your estimation, is so spot-on with its point-of-view and evidence-based conclusions that it's on a pedestal in your personal "hall of fame"?

Now here are some other questions: How unshakable is our knowledge of history? Is objectivity – the true ideal of the old-school journalist, at least, if not the real historian – really possible? Is our favorite foundational history merely the author's personal take, reconstructed in a neat, well-crafted, convincing narrative?

As the noted historian of history methodology, John Tosh, asks in *The Pursuit of History: Aims, Methods, and New Directions in the Study of History* (2015), "To ask questions about history is to enter the terrain of philosophy, since what is at issue is the nature of knowledge itself."[2]

In one chapter that addresses historical objectivity, Tosh ranges from explainer, to advocate, to devil's advocate, to critic, and back to advocate again on several schools of historical thought. Then he ruminates on why the ideal of objectivity is so elusive, and concludes with three "injunctions" to historians that will help belay distortion in interpretation and conclusions.[3] That chapter is the springboard for the discussion here.

The quest for objectivity has been one for the ages. Just in the last two centuries there have been the *19th-century positivist* position that history is a form of science in which historians amass facts derived from evidence; the *20th-century idealist* position that the imperfect and inherently subjective nature of the historical record is reason enough for historians to indulge their intuition and imagination; and the *postmodernist view* that challenges both positions with an agenda-driven approach.

In the view of John Tosh, there are three difficulties in the quest for objectivity: (1) Primary sources are an incomplete record, because "a great deal that happened left no material trace whatsoever." (2) Sources are tainted by less-than-pure intentions, because "the historical record is forever rigged in favor of the ruling class, which at all times has created the vast majority of the surviving sources." (3)

The Micro-Historian's Guide to
RESEARCH, EVIDENCE, & CONCLUSIONS — Formulation of Conclusions

The profusion of sources, as incomplete and sullied as they may be, is unmanageable, especially in the last century.[4]

Both the descriptive history of 19th-century historicists and the analytical history of 20th-century social historians take the heat from Tosh as the devil's advocate: "Most of what pass for the 'facts' of history actually depend on inference," he writes, noting that historians cannot observe facts the way a physicist can. "Formal proof may be beyond reach; what matters is the validity of the inferences." As for analytical history, which aims to convey understanding of abstractions, Tosh notes that its practitioners are more selective of supportive facts. "The facts are not given, they are selected. Despite appearances, they are never left to speak for themselves."[5]

If we throw our hands up in the air over the unattainability of pure objectivity, we can at least move on to improving our selection of facts. We must remember the simple truism that there are two kinds of history: (1) what really happened; and (2) the written history of what happened. "The facts of the *past* are limitless, while the facts of *history* are *selected* for reconstruction and explanation," writes Tosh, who opines that no historian approaches sources with a completely open mind, as the acquisition of context in secondary sources, so essential to research, may actually introduce bias.[6]

While objectivity remains the ideal of the *real* journalist writing "the first draft of history," for academic historians on the Ph.D. track, the pressure to pursue a fresh interpretation sometimes pushes that ideal to the side. At the most extreme is the approach of postmodernist historical presentism, in which some historians, claiming the assumed moral and intellectual high ground of the present, selectively choose their facts and omit selected context in order to advance a particular social or political viewpoint. Tosh, in fact, invokes the example of a historian who writes about the acknowledged horrors of the slave trade and the villainy of of its Anglo-Saxon perpetrators, yet resolutely omits any reference to the slave-market participation and complicity of West African societies at the time. As Tosh sternly notes, "Such distortions make for poor history."[7]

Is true *objectivity* unattainable because the *past* is equally unattainable? If we strive to present the history from a sensitive, context-aware point of view of the people who were there, whose point of view do we use? Rich or poor? Perpetrators or victims? And who is who? Then there is the problem of hindsight, because in history, we know (or think we know) what happened next. Our interpretation of an event in history cannot escape that influence. What to do?[8]

The three "injunctions." Paraphrased here are the three "injunctions" of John Tosh to history practitioners so they might avoid distortion: (1) Historians should strive for self-awareness of their own assumptions and values. (2) The research inquiry should be cast as an explicit hypothesis – to be accepted, rejected, or modified in light of the evidence. (3) Historians must always submit to the historical context, and respect both supporting and contrary evidence.[9]

Because of the nature of historical inquiry, there will always be multiple interpretations. But if history was uncontested, there would not be the raw material of critical debate on important social issues. John Tosh himself, the champion of rigorous standards, opines that "the past will never be beyond controversy; nor should it be."[10]

So, the history researcher may interpret evidence in hand-jotted notes, in a summary narrative, or in an award-winning book. But although the evidence may illuminate a subject in admirable detail, it may not be so "conclusive" that the historian's interpretation can answer every question. Future research – and future researchers – may uncover new evidence, and a fresh interpretation may answer long-standing questions, or pose new ones.

The research summary or reader-focused narrative, then, however "conclusive" it may or may not be, is shaped by (1) the nature of the research inquiry, (2) the aggregated evidence, and (3) the individual writer's approach to historic interpretation.

The next section is a brief introduction to the major theories and thinkers of history through the years, a sort of "Historiography Light." This overview leads to a more expansive discussion of microhistory, a tight-and-sharp-focus approach that has attained legitimacy in recent decades, especially in local history, genealogy, popular culture, and special interest research.

Historiography and Interpretation

Historiography is the fancy word for the study of the theory and practice of history, or how history is written and interpreted. The following overview breezes through the topic beginning with Herodotus in ancient Greece.[11] When choosing your approach to historic interpretation, you can pick your mentor and climb up on your favorite giant's shoulders.

• **Herodotus** (c. 484-424 B.C.E.), commonly referred to as "the father of history," distinguished his work by his commitment to reporting verifiable events instead of proliferating myths, and for

The Micro-Historian's Guide to
RESEARCH, EVIDENCE, & CONCLUSIONS   *Formulation of Conclusions*

linking ideas and probing for causality. His only known work, *The Histories* (440 BCE), is a study of the Greco-Persian Wars.

• **Thucydides** (c. 460-395 B.C.E.), also in ancient Greece, and sometimes called "the father of scientific history," made his mark through his standards of impartiality, evidence analysis, and emphasis on the political life of history's actors. most notably in his *History of the Peloponnesian War* (431-404 BCE).

• **Ibn Khaldun** (1332-1406), born in Tunisia, was a student of ancient Greek historiography, but expanded his view considerably, introducing a scientific approach to evaluating sources from the past. *Al-Muqaddimah*, the first of his seven-volume *Book of Lessons* is credited with introducing the disciplines of sociology, economics, and demography, as well as his highly-developed philosophy of history.[12]

• **Jean Mabillon** (1632-1707), a French Maurist monk, established the scholarly specialty of "diplomatics," which is the study of official government documents, charters, and manuscripts – and their seals, paper, signatures, and lettering styles – to determine primary source authenticity. His definitive work on the subject is *De re diplomatica* (1681).

• **Voltaire** (1694-1778), the French writer and philosopher, was also a groundbreaking Enlightenment-era historian, breaking free of antiquarianism and history centered around wars and generals. His history writing, exemplified in his *Essay on the Customs and the Spirit of the Nations* (1756), emphasized economics, politics, the arts, and social/cultural influences.[13]

• **Edward Gibbon** (1737-1794) of England set the bar high for historians in 1776 with the publication of his six-volume work, *The History of the Decline and Fall of the Roman Empire*. A stickler for the objective use of primary sources, Gibbon has been called "the first modern historian."

• **Jules Michelet** (1798-1874) was among the 19th-century movement of French historians advocating an approach to history that looked beyond the procession of royalty and the machinations of government. His 19-volume *Histoire de France* (1855) encompassed the history of the common people across the entire geography of France, and not just the "great men" of Paris.

• **Leopold von Ranke** (1795-1886) of Germany was an admired role model for European historians in the 19th century. He thought outside the usual parameters for the time, and greatly expanded the range of sources consulted by historians. For example, his own research for *The History of the Latin and Teutonic Peoples from 1494 to 1514* (1824), gathered evidence from memoirs, diaries, letters, government documents, and first-person accounts. More important was his rigorous analysis of documents to ascertain authenticity.

- **Marc Bloch** (1886-1944) of France was a co-founder, with Lucien Lebvre in the 1920s, of a new approach to historical thought that placed emphasis on social history, geography, and technology instead of politics and war. Bloch and his followers introduced quantitative analysis of populations of everyday people to the interpretation of history. His thoughts on the subject are in *The Historian's Craft* (1949), an unfinished work published posthumously that has influenced historians ever since.[14]

- **Fernand Braudel** (1902-1985) of France advanced the Annales school of thought developed by Bloch and Lebvre, and introduced the ideas of the "motionless history" of geography; the "long duration history" of social, political, and economic structures; and the "contextual history" of people and events. In Braudel's view, geography, climate, and demography are the most influential historical continuities, with short-term upheavals of secondary significance. His work pointed up the influence of socioeconomic factors on the course of history, and devoted much research to the scarcely documented populations of rural peasants and urban poor. In addition to his major works on European history, he wrote essays on historiography, collected in *On History* (1982).[15]

- **Donald Lines Jacobus** (1887-1970), born in Connecticut, is the lone genealogist on this short list of history thinkers. He has been called "the father of scientific genealogy" for his insistence on the use of primary sources, properly documented and cited, in genealogical research ... and for his obsession with rooting out family mythology and prideful puffery from the historical record. More than a theorist, Jacobus was a prolific genealogist and author whose principles and scholarly rigor are apparent in all of his works. Still useful and relevant today is *Genealogy as a Pastime and Profession* (1930, 1968).[16]

- **Eric Hobsbawm** (1917-2012) of England specialized in the long-view history of European industrial capitalism, socialism, and nationalism, through the prism of Marxist historiography. In *The Invention of Tradition* (1983), with T. O. Ranger, Hobsbawm explored the paradoxical equivalence of "invented traditions" and modernity, and its impact on nationalism.[17]

- **Laurel Thatcher Ulrich** (b. 1938) of the U.S. has been a successful exponent of microhistory in her studies of the lives of ordinary people within the context of their time and place. Among her many works, *A Midwife's Tale* (1990), a history based on the primary source of a late-18th-century New England midwife's diary, was awarded the Pulitzer and Bancroft prizes.[18]

- **Alan Taylor** (b. 1955) of the U.S. specializes in early United States history, and is known for his use of diaries, letters, court records, and land records – usually the comfort zone of genealogists – in his multi-disciplinary microhistory studies of people and places of the American past. Two of his narrative histories have received the Pulitzer prize: *William Cooper's Town: Power and Persuasion on the Frontier of the Early American Republic* (1995); and *The Internal Enemy: Slavery and War in Virginia, 1772-1832* (2013).[19]

20th-century history approaches in the U.S. In the U.S., the "progressive history" approach of the early 20th century defined American history through its capitalism and class conflict. The "consensus history" approach of the mid 20th century defined American history through its supposed acceptance of capitalism as the natural order of humankind. The "new left history" of the 1960s-1970s defined American history through race and class conflict. The "new social history" approach of the late 20th century to the present defines American history through the lives of ordinary people in historical, geographical, cultural, technological, and economic context. The "cultural history" approach of the late 20th century to the present defines American history through an anthropology-influenced view of cultural symbols, language, rituals, and societal values. Current postmodernist history appears to view the past from a historical presentist moral high ground.[20]

21st-Century Microhistory

The historical approach of microhistory is a subset of social history that focuses on tightly-defined units of research, such as on a particular individual, a particular town, or a singular event in time. The subject individual might be a relatively ordinary citizen, the town might be unremarkable, and the event might have affected relatively few people. But microhistory studies serve to enhance historical understanding, in that they allow us to see how the "micro" findings fit into the "macro" history context – or depart from it. Because ordinary people and events are not as well documented as generals and wars, in microhistory research there is often an absence of evidence due to a dearth of sources. The challenges for the micro-historian, therefore, are (1) crafting a narrative that navigates the gaps in research, perhaps even weaving in the obstacles of unanswered questions; and (2) arriving at an interpretation of evidence – and non-evidence – that is absolutely clear about what is known and unknown. Micro or macro, the responsible historian may posit clearly-labeled conjecture, but it must be derived from the rigorous and dispassionate analysis of evidence.

Microhistory defined. The term "microhistory" was embraced in the 1970s by its early practitioners in Italy, most notably Carlo Ginzburg (b. 1939) and Giovanni Levi (b. 1939), although the word showed up sporadically in theoretical writings for at least a decade before. In 1976, Ginzburg completed his book, *The Cheese and the Worms: The Cosmos of a 16th-Century Miller*, which became a touchstone of microhistory practice; and from 1981 to 1991, Levi, Ginzburg, and others edited the 21-book series, *Microstoria*, each book by 21 individual authors being a narrowly-focused local study of a particular historical episode.[21] Ginzburg himself, after decades of ruminations – and give-and-take with colleagues – described microhistory in 1993 as a way of studying isolated events, individuals, or actions, using close observation of small details; hearing every voice in a historical event; noting the gaps in documentation; and incorporating both hypotheses and methodology into the narrative.[22] Levi defined microhistory as "essentially based on the reduction of the scale of observation, on a microscopic analysis, and an intensive study of the documentary material."[23] In the decades since the formalization of the term, the definition continues to be refined and expanded by historians as well as theorists, its essence still the small scale of investigation and inclusion of the research process.

Microhistory origins. The first stirrings of microhistory in the 1970s were in reaction to the limitations of the still-new macrohistorical social science history. The new wave of microhistorians in Europe believed that the "little people" of history were being neglected just as much in the cool new analytical social science history, as they were in older approaches to political history that concentrated on the "high-and mighty."[24] Microhistory, as the new cultural history, has been described as "the rebellious child" of the new social history, in that "it was only after the new social history unseated older traditions of history writing which had privileged great men, great ideas, and great events, that historians could safely return to questions about ideas, meaning, language, and culture."[25]

Microhistory theory. The theory of microhistory developed in the 1970s-1980s from several schools of historical thought in Italy and Germany that shared the same basic outlook, but preferred a different emphasis. For example, leading history thinker Fernand Braudel, in *The Structures of Everyday Life: Civilization & Capitalism 15th-18th Century* (1967), explored the pre-industrial world in minute detail, incorporating "thick description" of social, structural, and economic context. But the cluster of pioneering microhistorians in Italy thought that the anthropology-oriented "thick description" group cultural approach to the study of everyday history did not go far enough.[26] Reactive to the analytical social sciences, microhistorians like Carlo Ginzburg and Giovanni Levi wanted to put human faces into history, and chronicle the life experiences of concrete human beings. They contended that generalizations derived from statistics do not necessarily dovetail with the reality of the lives the social scientist historian claims to explain.[27]

Carlo Ginzburg himself describes how he came to his mature microhistory approach in his 1993 article in the journal *Critical Inquiry*, modestly entitled "Microhistory: Two or Three Things That I Know About It." In describing his conception for *The Cheese and the Worms* (1976), he explains that he chose not to restrict himself to a descriptive reconstruction of an individual event, but instead he chose to narrate it. "Before beginning *The Cheese and the Worms* I had mulled over at length the relationship between research hypotheses and narrative strategies. I had set out to reconstruct the intellectual, moral, and fantastic world of the miller Menocchio on the basis of sources generated by persons who sent him to the stake." Ginzburg felt that it was possible to fill in the gaps in documentation and produce a convincing narrative, but chose instead to make the gaps part of his interpretation. "The obstacles interfering with the research were constituent elements of the documentation and thus had to become part of the account; the same for the hesitations and silences of the protagonist in the face of his persecutors' questions – or mine. Thus, the hypotheses, the doubts, the uncertainties became part of the narration; the search for truth became part of the exposition of the necessarily incomplete truth attained."[28]

Giovanni Levi has stated that he finds the most engaging models of microhistory to be those that emphasize the freedom of choice of ordinary people, and "their capacity to exploit the inconsistencies or incoherence of social and political systems to find loopholes through which they can wriggle or interstices in which they can survive."[29]

The Micro-Historian's Guide to
RESEARCH, EVIDENCE, & CONCLUSIONS   *Formulation of Conclusions*

As it has developed from Ginzburg's early example, microhistory presents both findings and procedure. "Microhistory accepts the limitations (of the unknown or unknowable)," Ginzburg wrote, "while exploring their gnoseological implications and transforming them into a narrative element."[30]

The early microhistorians in the 1970s were most comfortable exploring pre-modern communities. But more recent microhistorians have explored political and social conflicts in the 20th century. In Germany, the microhistory approach of *Alltagsgeschichte*, or "everyday history" advanced by Alf Ludtke (b. 1943) and others, has probed subjects and questions that have defied more conventional large-scale social science analysis. Practitioners of *Alltagsgeschichte* contend that it must have macrohistorical context. Most notable are the studies of Alf Ludtke and Lutz Neithammer of the working classes in Nazi Germany, and their still-puzzling support and participation in the buildup and eventual horrors of WWII.[31]

The *Alltagsgeschichte* approach is outlined in Alf Ludtke's introduction to the anthology *The History of Everyday Life* (1989). "What *Alltagsgeschichte* is and the uses it serves remains a matter of spirited debate, not just among historians," Ludtke writes. "In doing the history of everyday life, attention is focused not just on the deeds (and misdeeds) and pageantry of the great, the masters of church and state. Rather, central to the thrust of everyday historical analysis is the life and survival of those who have remained anonymous in history – the nameless multitudes in their workaday trials and tribulations, and their occasional outbursts."[32]

Ludtke notes that "everyday history" studies of the Nazi period in Germany have been reverberating and sometimes controversial. "These investigations attempt to give back a human face to the victims of German fascism – the hounded, exploited, and murdered millions. ... Inquiry into the history of everyday life points up the extent to which most 'average people' actually clung to the Nazi regime in their concern to survive. In the end, it was the 'others' who bore the cost of that process."[33]

In Ludtke's example of the much-studied Nazi era in Germany, microhistory is an essential supplement to earlier social science macrohistory, not a repudiation. So macrohistory and microhistory should not clash, but rather inform and extend each other. Microhistory serves to test macrohistory constructs against existing reality on a small scale.[34]

George G. Iggers, in *Historiography in the Twentieth Century* (1997), brings his opinion to the fore when addressing microhistory: "There is no reason why a history dealing with broad social transformations, and one centering on individual existences, cannot co-exist and supplement each other. It should be the task of the historian to explore the connections between these two levels of historical experience."[35]

Applicability of microhistory. The work of Ginzburg, Ludtke, and others in the late 20th century has shown that the microhistory approach is applicable to interpreting significant historical periods of the recent past as well as the distant past. In more recent times, the microhistory approach has proven applicable to local history, special interest history, and family history. In studies of local history, the microhistory approach fills out the macro social and cultural abstractions in smaller-scale human detail, breathing life into generalizations.[36]

In special interest history topics, which may range from narrowly-defined aspects of domestic life, to thinly-sliced studies of particular technology, tools, crafts, trades, occupations, folk art, decorative arts, implements, ornaments, foodways, fashion, leisure, popular culture, and more, the microhistory approach encourages penetration below the surface that sometimes reveals previously unknown connections. In topics from philandery to philately, it is almost routine for a micro-study to reveal surprisingly interwoven relationships through art, science, culture, ... and individuals. Examples within this genre, which defines microhistory more broadly than purists might prefer, are *One Good Turn: A Natural History of the Screwdriver and the Screw* (2000), by Witold Rybczynski; *Seeds of Change: Six Plants That Transformed Mankind* (2005), by Henry Hobhouse; and *A History of the World in Six Glasses* (2005), by Tom Standage. This genre owes much to science historian James Burke (b. 1936) and his BBC television documentary series and book, *Connections* (1978).

Family history research projects and individual genealogy research projects are ideal for the microhistory approach. The micro approach is suitable for presenting the minutiae of an individual's life in context, regardless of whether that individual was at the center of local, regional, or national historical context ... or on the fringe. And according to some microhistory theorists, it is not absolutely necessary to relate the life details of a research subject to wider historical context or to generalities based on social science data analysis.

Genealogist Anne Rodda, author of *Trespassers in Time: Genealogists and Microhistorians* (2012), presents a convincing argument for the use of the microhistory approach in genealogy. In her doctoral research for the Drew University program in Irish Studies, after her study of various methodologies, she determined that the microhistory approach is "perfectly suited to the genealogist who wishes to go beyond the charts. It is the most promising route to understanding the lives of individuals and families in specific times and places."[37]

Dr. Rodda bases much of her rationale for the appropriateness of microhistory for genealogy on the theoretical writings of Sigurdur Gylfi Magnusson (b. 1957), longtime chair of the Centre for Microhistory Research at Reykjavik Academy. In *What is Microhistory?* (2012), he explains that "The microhistorians placed their emphasis on small units and how people conducted their lives within them. By reducing the scale of observation, microhistorians argue that they are more likely to reveal the complicated function of individual relationships within each and every social setting, and they stressed its difference from larger norms. Microhistorians tend to focus on outliers rather than looking for the average individual as found by the application of quantitative research methods. Instead, they scrutinize those individuals who did not follow the paths of their average fellow countryman, thus making them their focal point."[38]

In synthesizing her understanding of microhistory, Dr. Rodda arrived at her own definition applied to genealogy work that describes microhistory as a way of studying a specific time and place, and the experience of ordinary people in it. That study may include observations of relationships and interactions in small social settings, and involves scrutiny of all types of evidence, sometimes little evidence, all of which may combine and result in multiple interpretations.[39]

Microhistory caveats & concerns. The microhistory approach has not been beyond criticism. In *Historiography in the Twentieth Century*, George Iggers notes that criticisms have included reducing history to "anecdotal antiquarianism, romanticizing past cultures, inability to apply the method to more rapidly changing modern times, and unsuitability for dealing with politics."[40] Critics of the Ludtke and Niethammer *Alltagsgeschichte* Nazi studies have voiced concern that by focusing on the everyday aspects of life in 1930s Germany that continued relatively undisturbed, such a focus may normalize the image of the Nazi regime.[41] Microhistory advocate Anne Rodda cautions genealogists to be wary of tradition or nostalgia creeping into microhistory work, which invariably results in distorted conclusions.[42]

Microhistory "in the final analysis". "In the final analysis," writes George Iggers, "microhistory appears not as a negation of a history of broader social contexts, but as a supplement to it."[43] Carlo

Ginzburg concurs that microhistory does not exist in a vacuum apart from broader historical context and other historical approaches: "In all institutions, innovations, in fact ruptures with the past, make headway by means of the reaffirmation of a certain continuity with what has gone before."[44] He notes that the observations in a microhistory study may or may not relate to a broader context. "The results obtained in a microscopic sphere cannot be automatically transferred to a macroscopic sphere, and vice versa. The heterogeniety, the implications of which we are just beginning to perceive, constitutes both the greatest difficulty and the greatest potential benefit of microhistory."[45]

Conclusions Interpret Change, Continuity, and Causality

In common to all of the approaches to history outlined above, microhistory included, are the historian's research and interpretation of change, continuity, and causality. Distinguishing every approach to history is the individual historian's view of our human existence: Is history linear? Or is it a cycle of patterns? Is history a predictable or inevitable progression? Or is it a regression? What is the right balance of "great man" history to "common people" history? Before the mid-19th century, the "great man" approach to history prevailed, with emphasis on political events and wars. By the early 20th century the "ordinary people" were in the history books, as new approaches to history encompassed economics, industrialism, capitalism, and labor. In the latter half of the 20th century, the social/cultural approach to history expanded into related humanities and social science disciplines to explore history from previously untold points of view. Statistics revealed trends and truths. And now micro-studies reveal the richness and the individual choice of the "outliers." Some postmodernist historians believe that historians should filter their work through an enlightened moral agenda, and feel justified, from a presentist's point of 21st-century presumed intellectual high ground, to recast history by the selective exclusion of context. What should be their place on the continuum of the craft? Have they gone too far? Or not far enough?

Conclusions ... and change. All historians, even microhistorians focused on a one-hour or one-day period, in some way study and interpret change over time. In the linear model, historians view change as a progression to an inevitable end. In the history of past centuries, this linear conception of change suggested that humankind was progressing to an improved, enlightened future. Nationalist-oriented histories extended this conception with a belief that a particular nation or culture would enjoy indefinite stability. In the cyclical model, historians view change as patterns that tend to repeat themselves. Perhaps it is no accident that the cyclical view of history – i.e. a once vigorous culture reaching the heights before its inevitable decay – has been embraced during times of conflict and pessimism. A third model of change posits that some changes occur so slowly that they are imperceptible to the individuals who experience them, and only become visible to historians in retrospect. This concept allows historians to detect, from a retrospective big-picture viewpoint, moments of reaction or innovation. The ultimate change model for macrohistory may be the study of climate change and its impact throughout the millenia. In formulating conclusions from evidence relating to change, beware of being unconsciously influenced by "conventional wisdom" that is based on too overly optimistic or pessimistic models of change. Other than the change model potential of climatology, keep in mind that the linear and cyclical change models are historian-imposed mental constructs, not discovered realities.[46]

Conclusions ... and continuity. All historians that have ever put pen to paper or pounded a keyboard have addressed the notion of continuity, because in a history narrative, the continuity of the setting, time, and place provides the rhythm-of-life underpinning to gradual, cyclical, or cataclysmic change. The various conceptions of continuity parallel the models of change above, therefore in formulating conclusions from evidence relating to continuity, the same caution applies.

Conclusions ... and causality. All historians address causality in some way. In fact, the very act of assembling a basic chronology of events implies a causal relationship to at least some small degree. In observing and addressing change in history, cataclysmic or infinitesimal, the historian looks for a cause. Unfortunately there is no simple formula for determining cause in history. And there are many cautions and questions: Is cause knowable? Is what is initially perceived as "cause" really just a convenient "correlation" of events or facts? Is what is initially perceived as a "cause" instead really a "motive" (i.e. motivating event) but not a direct cause? Might there be primary and secondary causes? Have complexities of causes been considered? Have the multiple "causal factors" been ranked for analysis? And what was the rationale for the ranking? Do you have a headache yet? To the rescue come authors Martha Howell and Walter Prevenier, who in *From Reliable Sources* (2001) categorize the basic categories of causal factors that historians, macro and micro, should be sure to consider: (1) religious idealogy (or aversion to same); (2) social & economic; (3) biology & race; (4) environment; (5) science, technology, & invention; (6) power; and (7) public opinion/mass media.[47] One category to add to the above list of causal factors is that of an individual actor in a historical event. While the trend in history writing at present is to focus on the effect of larger causal forces on everyday people, and in microhistory, to focus on the lives of "the little people" in small groups, the fact remains that at times it is an individual – and not necessarily a genius, general, or CEO – that changes the course of history. In formulating conclusions from evidence relating to causality, consider *all* the possible causes. Remember that correlation is not cause. And that life, even before you were in it, could be complicated.

Conclusions ... in messy practice. After the following discussion of the conclusions in practice, and issues that may arise, it is onward, in the next chapter, to their expression in the summary narrative.

Some practical issues in the formulation of conclusions:

• **19th-century Colonial Revivalism and 21st-century historical presentism in the history of indigenous people in Middletown, Conn.** In 2004 your author became editor of *The Middler*, the quarterly journal-of-record of the Society of Middletown (Conn.) First Settlers Descendants. Before assuming the position I determined topics to explore, including Puritanism, material culture, domestic life, architecture, agriculture, economics, social services, public infrastructure, English origins, western destinations, research resources, notable local historians, Middletown's maritime involvement in the West Indies trade, and African-Americans and Native Americans in Middletown. The first decade of research also culminated in the book, *Early Families of Middletown, Conn. – Vol. I:1650-1654* (2012)[48].

The two-part *Middler* series on Native Americans in Middletown (2010) was well-received, later republished in the book, and in 2013 selected for inclusion in Yale University's scholarly *Indian Papers* project. The series on the indigenous Wangunk tribe of central Connecticut surveyed what was known and written about their presence in the region, and their interactions with newly-arrived settlers. As expected, my survey revealed marginalization, swindling, and cruel indignities, as well as collaboration, cooperation, and simple indifference.

My overriding "conclusion" based on writings since 1650 was that Native Americans in Middletown have had little opportunity to speak for themselves. In fact, late-19th-century historians commonly wrote Native Americans out of the local history. [A fine reference, published shortly after my research on the Wangunks, is *Firsting and Lasting: Writing Indians Out of Existence in New England*, by Jean M. O'Brien (2010).[49]] Among my remarks on the marginalization of the region's indigenous people: "We seldom have the Native Americans speaking for themselves in telling their story. It is mostly a parade of myopic observers, breathless apologists, dreamy myth-makers, and agenda-driven revisionists, along with the honest interpreters."[50]

In fall 2015, a professor at Wesleyan University in Middletown, Kehaulani Kawanui, in an admirable use of local history, focused on the Native American and early-settler relationships in Middletown as an area of study in a course entitled "Decolonizing Indigenous Middletown: Native Histories of the Wangunk Indian People." My writings as referenced in the *Yale Indian Papers* were assigned as required reading so that students would have background context prior to their research in primary source records. In late 2015 I was invited to speak at a seminar at Wesleyan University on the subject along with two historical archaeologists with insights on thousands of years of Native American life in the region, and a descendant of Middletown's indigenous population who has embraced the mantle of his surviving people. The audience was made up of the general public, plus the students in the professor's class. Individual speaker presentations were followed by a panel discussion.

The presentations of the panelists were enlightening to the audience, and to each other. Dr. Lucianne Lavin summarized her decades of research on the indigenous people of central Connecticut. Wangunk descendant Gary O'Neil spoke passionately and eloquently about his family history as passed down from elders. In my presentation, as a representative of the descendants' organization as well as a historian, I was immediately forthright about the early arrivals – my own ancestors – being the "first exploiters" of the indigenous people of Middletown and expressed my jaundiced view of hereditary organizations that seem to exist in order to re-assert Anglo-Saxon preeminence, and that the group I represented was not one of them. Dr. Timothy Ives focused on the differing views of land use and ownership between the new arrivals and the indigenous people. His research identified the systemic land-taking by the early white settlers that first pushed the Wangunks into designated reservations, and then through the decades effectively de-populated the reservation acreage.[51] This was a topic of particular interest to the students who had probed primary source records on the subject.

In the follow-up panel discussion, I knew that as the representative of the Middletown descendants' organization, I would be the designated bad guy despite my presentation content. I was taken to task by students who were perched firmly on the pinnacle of enlightened

21st-century moral high ground, first for semantics, and then for suggesting that to merely acknowledge context in historical studies is not to justify or be an apologist for wrongdoing. There was a certain irony in the student challenges, since it was my work that formed the basis for the students' contextual understanding of the subject in the first place. But of course I kept that to myself. In a subsequent report I was moved to paraphrase an observation by the late violinist Isaac Stern, expressing tolerance of his virtuoso students and their superheated interpretations: "Without the excesses in your formative stages, you have nothing to chisel away and discard as you sculpt the masterpiece of your maturity."[52]

This experience of my research aiding student discovery – and then my own advocacy for understanding being turned against me – prompts two warnings to neophyte historians who aim to formulate conclusions from research on indigenous people in Colonial-era settlements: (1) Do not blindly accept the writings of late-19th-century Colonial Revival dabblers who wrote Native Americans out of local history as authoritative context; and (2) Resist the lure of historical presentism, i.e. evaluating the people, events, and societal constructs of the past *only* through the values, beliefs, and advances of the present, without factoring in the context of the historical period. These warnings will help, but growing a thick alligator skin might help more as protection against the slings-and-arrows of political correctness.

- **Old news: Sometimes conclusions are dictated by external forces.** In the public history and museum field, sometimes the most comprehensive and objective evidence-based conclusions of research scholars wind up being re-shaped by external forces.

In 2009, a first-class team of historians, museum professionals, and exhibition designers was engaged to create a permanent exhibition on Boston's theatrical history for Emerson College's new development in the city's theatre district, the Paramount Center.[53] The plan was to have exhibition panels, archival images, maps, and atmospheric graphics spread throughout the public spaces of the $80-million complex. Completed in 2011, the project includes the re-imagined 590-seat Paramount Theatre, a black-box performance space, classrooms, studios, offices, and dormitory residences. In all, its area encompasses the footprint of a half-dozen of Boston's earliest theatres.

Your author was engaged to provide the vaudeville history component, along with images and graphics. This content was especially notable because the footprint of the Paramount Center is the very locus of vaudeville origins. Once located within the site on Boston's

Washington Street were the former Paramount Theatre (1932; 1700 seats), the Lion/Melodeon/Gaiety/Bijou Theatre (1836/1839/1878/1883; 1021 seats), B. F. Keith's New Theatre (1894; 1800 seats), the Adams House theatrical hotel (1850), and the storefront dime museum where in 1883 B. F. Keith and E. F. Albee first produced vaudeville shows on a backroom stage facing a cluster of 75 straight-back kitchen chairs.[54]

Boston's roots in 17th-century Puritanism ensured that theatre, music, and public amusement were looked down upon for the first hundred years of the city's history. But in 1795, John Bill Ricketts presented his equestrian circus in Boston, with his pavilion less than a hundred yards from the Paramount Center.[55] In 1846, Moses Kimball, an admirer of P. T. Barnum's American Museum in New York City, opened the Boston Museum on Tremont Street, which combined fine art, natural history specimens (including the "Fiji Mermaid"), and a 1600-seat theatre for dramatic spectacles and theatrical variety shows.[56]

While dramatic fare and musical recitals drew audiences in Boston, in the late 19th and early 20th century it was the popularity of general audience vaudeville that fueled the theatre district. In Boston and across the U.S., box-office proceeds financed construction of palatial 2000-seat vaudeville theaters in the largest cities, and more modest 600-seat theatres in smaller cities. Rural areas got their vaudeville from traveling shows at Grange halls, on showboats, or under tents. The vaudeville variety show – a program of six or eight "acts" unrelated by plot – was a staple on the cultural landscape in the U.S. for 50 years, roughly 1880-1930. Many of the finest performing artists in the world in all genres worked in "big-time" vaudeville, and earned big money. The beginnings of vaudeville were in Boston and New York, where entrepreneurs, enabled by advances in transportation and communication, booked all manner of music, dance, acrobatic, and novelty talent for 40-week tours on national or regional circuits of theatres.

The Paramount Center was exquisitely executed, and a credit to Emerson College. Although the Boston theatre history exhibition was only a small component of the project, its content and design were excellent. But the shrinking exhibit space as construction neared completion, plus the choice of emphasis by the ultimate decision-makers above our team, resulted in an adjusted interpretation of the history. To fully understand this adjustment, more context is in order.

Because at present we are a century removed from the cultural, economic, and artistic peak of vaudeville, the current public perception of the genre, if any, is built on stereotypes of vaudeville in old Hollywood movies rather than on evidence of history. Misconceptions

The Micro-Historian's Guide to
RESEARCH, EVIDENCE, & CONCLUSIONS   *Formulation of Conclusions*

include confusion with blackface minstrelsy or lowbrow burlesque; a belief that talent was marginal at best; and a belief that the theatres were all rat-infested hell-holes. Yes, there was plenty of mediocrity in small-time vaudeville. But in its day, mediocrity did not define the genre. Also, the cliche that "the talkies killed vaudeville," is the popular refrain, but actually the decline was due to a combination of internal and external factors in the 1930s. In the ensuing decades, Hollywood movies, in their depiction of vaudeville, helped burnish the misconceptions of the genre – another case of the victors writing the history.

As one of several popular culture researchers who have illuminated the misconceptions about vaudeville in an effort to tell the real story of that era in theatrical history, your author cited, for the Paramount Center project, mountains of evidence, including an economic study in 1923[57] that determined that attendance at vaudeville theatres outnumbered attendance at all orchestral concerts, music recitals, opera, ballet, and dramatic productions *combined* by a factor of ten-to-one.[58] In Boston and surrounding industrial cities, vaudeville ruled. In 1928 Boston boasted 14 vaudeville theatres. The centerpiece was the 2900-seat Keith Memorial Theatre. (Today this is known as the Opera House, on Washington Street adjacent to the Paramount Center.)

Our team wrapped up the comprehensive view of Boston's theatrical history interpretation in fine fashion, and the designers executed artful panels of text and graphics to fill the allotted 90 linear feet of display space in the public areas of the Paramount Center. Then, as the interior finish construction was coming together, architectural necessity reduced the display space from 90 linear feet to 75 feet ... then about two weeks later to 60 feet ... then to 45 feet ... and eventually to 29 feet, with tidbits of content squeezed into other nooks-and-crannies here-and-there. Nevertheless, the final product was a model of excellence and a point of pride for all involved.

But in the truncation of exhibition content, the story of vaudeville, which has so much of its early history within the footprint of the Paramount Center, was de-emphasized in favor of placing dramatic productions at the front-and-center of Boston's theatrical history. As the exhibition stands, it is well done, and it is probably the closest manifestation of a permanent museum-grade exhibition on Boston's theatrical history that will ever exist. But the interpretation chosen by the Emerson College decision-makers distorted the real story.

One might wonder if the higher-up decision-makers, at the 11th-hour of this project, thought it best to recast Boston's theatrical history in order to cater to the more dramatic-arts interests of deep-pockets donors and patrons of the "legitimate theatre" than to tell the real story of popular theatrical entertainment for the sweaty and swarthy masses. To be fair, however, it is likely that even the most astute decision-makers were themselves long ago inoculated with the entrenched misconceptions of vaudeville. After all, for several generations of academic theatrical historians as well as self-styled cultural critics, the entrenched misconceptions have been their *only* vaudeville context.

This report is old news to old veterans, but a heads-up to neophyte researchers who may be formulating conclusions on a project: That in museums and public history exhibitions, unfortunately sometimes it is the funding motive, the space motive, or the entrenched-beliefs motive that prevail over a researcher's dispassionate objectivity, and ultimately dictate the interpretation of history to the public.

- **When conclusions make you "Professor Buzzkill."** In 2017, in conjunction with the Newburyport (Mass.) Preservation Trust, a non-profit education and advocacy organization, your author completed a book, *The HABS and the HABs NOTs: Documenting the Architecture of Newburyport in the Historic Amerian Buildings Survey* (2017).[59] The book included a chapter on the history of the small coastal city from the point of view of a preservation advocate – but one who is also a no-nonsense historian with low tolerance for Colonial Revival baloney.

Because I choose to continue living in this city, preferably in peaceful relative anonymity, my research and writing of history is generally devoted to other topics and regions. But a book devoted to the city's early architecture would be incomplete without addressing the city's early history. Therefore, mindful of local historians and others of long tenure who appear to claim a protective ownership of the small-town history, I deliberately crafted the history chapter to stay above the fray: "This brief and broad overview of Newburyport history purpose-fully avoids identification of heroes, villains, brilliance, or ignorance."[60]

Newburyport, like many New England port cities, saw its economy flourish from the mid-18th-century until the Embargo Act of 1807. The riches that poured into Newburyport from the West Indies rum trade financed advances in infrastructure, education, literacy, trades, and craftsmanship. Today, architecture enthusiasts rhapsodize over the classic Georgian and Federal era homes in Newburyport originally built for sea captains and merchants. Overlooked is the other half of the story, distant and invisible in its time, that New England's economy in that period was built squarely on the backs of enslaved Africans at sugar cane plantations in the Caribbean. In other words, the stately Federal-era homes we admire today were financed by the slavery-driven "triangle trade" we learned about in junior high school. That fact is old news to history scholars[61], but in New England it is a fact slow to be embraced by local museums and historians, whose focus is usually on history that fosters local pride. Unfortunately, at many small museums across the U.S. that struggle to maintain membership, support, and a non-leaking roof, the mission of "telling the whole story" of history sometimes gives way to "history that pays the bills."

My view as a museum professional, historian, and former journalist, is that in my work I have a responsibility to the public to tell the whole story of history, not just the "feel-good" parts. But how does the local historian present uncomfortable facts of local history to a readership and local/regional population that has grown up with the belief that New Englanders were always the "good guys" in the slavery story?

In the book my approach to the slavery connection was fortified by the measured verbiage of maritime scholar Benjamin W. Labaree, in quoting from his masterful work, *New England and the Sea* (1972, 1994): "Historians of early New England have been slow to recognize how much of the region's prosperity depended upon the institution of slavery. ... The coffers of some of New England's finest families were filled with profits from this trade."[62] Bolstered by Dr. Labaree's legitimacy, I barreled into the evidence of Newburyport shipyards turning out purpose-built floating prisons for the slave trade that were sold to British customers.[63] Then the revelations were leavened with context.

When presenting messy history, adding companion context is advisable to avoid being "Professor Buzzkill." To be fair, to the average Newburyporter in the late 18th century, the degree of human suffering at Caribbean sugar cane plantations 1500 miles away could not be fully known. Unlike today, there were no real-time satellite video feeds. As for the merchants and sea captains, as Dr. Labaree pointed out, it is unfair for we moderns to cast the merchants as villains, when we live apart from the context of their times.[64] My contention is that it is possible to appreciate the design, engineering, creativity, ingenuity, hard labor, human energy, and exquisite craftsmanship that went into the merchant-class mansions; and *at the same time* openly acknowledge that it was the stolen labor of the enslaved that financed them.

But just as there is risk in bringing up messy history, there is also risk in bringing up its context. It is possible that a well-meaning critic from the moral high ground – at the opposite extreme from the Colonial Revival crowd – will regard the introduction of *any* context that explains the slavery-driven "triangle trade" as an attempt to justify it. So, to be a real historian, one might as well get comfortable being "Professor Buzzkill."

NOTES to Formulation of Conclusions

(1) Robert Charles Anderson. *Elements of Genealogical Analysis.* (Boston, Mass.: New England Historic Genealogical Society, 2014), pg. 58-59, 131.

(2) John Tosh. *The Pursuit of History: Aims, Methods, and New Directions in the Study of History* (6th ed.). (New York, N.Y.: Routledge, 2015), pg. 149.

(3) Ibid., pg. 148-179

(4) Ibid., pg. 152-153.

(5) Ibid., pg. 154.

(6) Ibid., pg. 154-156.

(7) Ibid., pg. 163.

(8) Ibid., pg. 164.

(9) Ibid., pg. 176.

(10) Ibid., pg. 176.

(11) Kenneth R. Stunkel. *Fifty Key Works of History and Historiography.* (New York, N.Y.: Routledge, 2011).

(12) Walter Fischel. *Ibn Khaldun in Egypt : His Public Functions and his Historical Research, 1382–1406.* (Berkeley, Calif.: University of California Press, 1967).

(13) J. H. Brumfitt. *Voltaire: Historian.* (London, England: Oxford University Press, 1958).

(14) Peter Burke. *The French Historical Revolution: The Annales School 1929–89.* (Malden, Mass., & Cambridge, England: Polity Press, 1990, 2015).

(15) Fernand Braudel. *On History.* (Chicago, Ill.: University of Chicago Press, 1980).

(16) Donald Lines Jacobus. *Genealogy as a Pastime and Profession.* (Baltimore, Md.: Genealogical Publishing Co., 1930, 1968).

(17) Eric Hobsbawm. *On History.* (New York, N.Y.: The New Press, 1997).

(18) Laurel Thatcher Ulrich. *A Midwife's Tale: The Life of Martha Ballard based on Her Diary, 1785–1812.* (New York, N.Y.: Alfred A. Knopf, Inc., 1990).

(19) Alan Taylor. *William Cooper's Town: Power and Persuasion on the Frontier of the Early American Republic.* (New York: Alfred A. Knopf, Inc., 1995).

(20) Martha Howell & John Prevenier. *From Reliable Sources: An Introduction to Historical Methods.* (Ithaca, N.Y.: Cornell U. Press, 2001), pg. 112-118; Tosh, pg. 162-163.

(21) Tosh, pg. 67

(22) Carlo Ginzburg. "Microhistory: Two or Three Things That I Know About It." *Critical Inquiry 20* (Fall 1993). (Chicago, Ill.: University of Chicago Press, 1993), pg. 10-35.

(23) Giovanni Levi. "On Microhistory," in Peter Burke, ed., *New Perspectives on Historical Writing.* (University Park, Pa.: Pennsylvania State University Press, 1992), pg. 95.

(24) Georg G. Iggers. *Historiography in the 20th Century: From Scientific Objectivity to the Postmodern Challenge.* (Hanover, N.H.: Univ. Press of New England, 1997), pg. 101-102.

(25) Howell & Prevenier, pg. 115.

(26) Iggers, pg. 101-117.

(27) Ibid., pg. 108

(28) Ginzburg, pg. 23-24

(29) Levi, pg. 16.

(30) Ibid., pg. 28

(31) Iggers, pg. 114.

(32) Alf Ludtke, ed. *The History of Everyday Life: Reconstructing Historical Experiences and Ways of Life.* (Princeton, N.J.: Princeton University Press, 1989), pg. 3-4.

(33) Ibid., pg. 4.

(34) Iggers, pg. 110.
(35) Iggers, pg. 104.
(36) Tosh, pg. 67-68.
(37) Anne P. Rodda. *Trespassers in Time: Genealogists and Microhistorians.* (Middletown, Del.: Rodda Publications, 2012), pg. 4.
(38) Sigurdur Gylfi Magnusson and István M. Szijarto. *What is Microhistory?: Theory and Practice.* (New York, N.Y.: Routledge, 2013).
(39) Rodda, pg. 74-75.
(40) Iggers, pg. 113.
(41) Ibid., pg. 115
(42) Rodda, pg. 19-20.
(43) Iggers, pg. 117.
(44) Ginzburg, pg. 19.
(45) Ibid., pg 33.
(46) Howell & Prevenier, pg. 119-127.
(47) Ibid., pg. 131-141.
(48) R. W. Bacon. *Early Families of Middletown, Conn., Vol. I: 1650-1654.* (Newburyport, Mass.: Variety Arts Press, 2012), pg. 117-132.
(49) Jean M. O'Brien. *Firsting and Lasting: Writing Indians Out of Existence in New England.* (Minneapolis, Minn.: University of Minnesota Press, 2010).
(50) R. W. Bacon. *Early Families of Middletown, Conn., Vol. I: 1650-1654,* pg. 130.
(51) R. W. Bacon. "Mattabesett Wangunk tribe is finally in the spotlight ...". *The Middler* (spring 2016). (Newburyport, Mass.: Soc. of Middletown First Settlers Desc., 2016), pg. 3-5.
(52) Ibid., pg. 10.
(53) R. W. Bacon. Research and consultation for Emerson College, Boston, Mass. in 2009, for the vaudeville component of its permanent exhibition on Boston's theatrical history displayed throughout the Paramount Center, 559 Washington St., Boston, Mass.
(54) Donald C. King. *The Theatres of Boston: A Stage & Screen History* (Jefferson, N.C.: MacFarland & Co., 2005).
(55) John T. Prince. "Boston's Lanes and Alleys," (a paper presented October 9, 1888) in *Publications of the Bostonian Society, Vol. 7.* (Boston, Mass.: The Bostonian Society, 1888).
(56) King, pg. 32-36.
(57) Alfred L. Bernheim. "Equity News", Sept. 1923 to March 1924, in *Equity Magazine*, (New York, N.Y.: Actors' Equity).
(58) Donald B. Wilmeth, *Variety Entertainment and Outdoor Amusements: A Reference Guide.* (Westport, Conn.: Greenwood Press, 1982), pg.132-133.
(59) R. W. Bacon. *The HABS and the HABs NOTs: Documenting the Architecture of Newburyport in the Historic American Buildings Survey.* (Newburyport, Mass.: Variety Arts Press, 2017), pg. 7-10.
(60) Ibid., pg. 7.
(61) Benjamin W. Labaree. *Patriots and Partisans: The Merchants of Newburyport 1764-1815.* (Cambridge, Mass.: Harvard University Press, 1962).
(62) Robert G. Albion, William A. Baker, & Benjamin W. Labaree. *New England and the Sea.* (Mystic, Conn.: Mystic Seaport Museum, 1972, 1994), pg. 37.
(63) Susan M. Harvey. *Slavery in Massachusetts: A Descendant of Early Settlers Investigates the Connections in Newburyport, Mass.* (Fitchburg State U. thesis, 2011).
(64) Albion, Baker, & Labaree. *New England and the Sea,* pg. 53.

The Micro-Historian's Guide to
RESEARCH, EVIDENCE, & CONCLUSIONS   *The Summary Narrative*

A History Writer's Checklist

✓ **Assemble completed research-to-date.** Assemble your evidence derived from research, along with source citations, and any accompanying analysis, conclusions, or commentary. *(See pg. 10-73.)*

✓ **Use your writer's toolkit.** Keep your writer's toolkit handy, at the minimum a dictionary, a grammar guide, and a stylebook ... preferably in thumb-able hard-copy format. *(See pg. 82.)*

✓ **Know your "story."** What is it about your assembled evidence that grabs *your* interest? What *should* hold reader interest? Of all the "who, what, when, where, why, and how" questions, which one arouses the most curiosity? Does your history "story" have interesting patterns, connections, relationships, myth-bustings, or man-bites-dog incongruities? Tell your story to tolerant friends, and note what details resonate. You can't write your "story" if you don't know what it is.

✓ **Know your reading audience.** Will you have "motivated readers" already interested in the topic? Or will you have "general readers" of varying contextual knowledge ... and attention spans? Anticipate the "So what?" and "Who cares?" questions.

✓ **Make an outline.** Think first ... and then get organized with a written plan to tell your history story. *(See pg. 76-81.)* If your content seems too complicated, get started with the "introduction-content-summary" approach used in public speaking: "Tell 'em what your gonna tell 'em. Then tell 'em. Then tell 'em what you told 'em."

✓ **Write your history "story"... by following your outline.** Get the "story" down according to plan, in your own voice. Then read it aloud.

✓ **Polish the jewel.** Revise your history "story" with attention to language. Enrich the narrative, when appropriate, with verbiage that conveys mood and atmosphere. Use active voice. Don't be a wimp. Don't be a bore. It is not a crime to keep readers awake. *(See pg. 83.)*

✓ **Edit & proofread.** Don't skimp onn this steppe. *(See pg. 84-85.)*

✓ **Format footnotes/endnotes & bibliography.** Comprehensive documentation of sources is essential. *(See pg. 103-104.)*

The Summary Narrative

It is so energizing, not to mention so much fun, when you are deep "in the zone" with historical of genealogical research. Mountains of information pile up, and of course you keep it organized and documented in your research log, right? It is probably true for every history or genealogy research project that the researcher has not accumulated enough data until they have much more of it than they can ever use. But at some point it is time to summarize, if not for a magisterial book or a groundbreaking article, at least to keep the research findings of a sprawling work-in-progress clear in the mind. For many individuals, that point of sitting down to write is a point of utter dread. The hope is that this chapter will moderate some of the pain, cushion the craggy path, and provide guidance to a well-crafted and useful finished product.

Conceiving the Narrative

Whatever the historical theory approach embraced in the conception of the summary narrative, there are several truisms to contemplate:

- **We humans like stories.** Historians can tell very specific mico-stories as well as expansive big-picture stories. At best the little stories and the big stories inform each other. In all good histories, macro or micro, the storytelling historian finds ways in the narrative to make the ordinary extraordinary.

- **We humans like to hang on to our favorite myths.** Be warned. If you write enough objective, dispassionate history, you will, at some point, write something that somebody does not like because it does not conform to their myopic world view. This hazard goes with the territory, so you might as well embrace it.

- **We humans like patterns.** Every approach to history favors evidence and facts that illustrate patterns. But be mindful that in history, correlation is not necessarily cause; and the specific does not necessarily extrapolate to the general. Interpretation within the narrative must be based on sound reasoning.

- **We humans like departures from patterns.** It may appear counter-intuitive, but microhistories can actually enhance big-picture understanding when they tell the story of the "outliers," or the "other."

- **We humans are multi-dimensional.** And so is our history. Today's historians incorporate, when relevant to their topic, all disciplines in the humanities, social sciences, and physical sciences.

- **Historians ply a craft.** Whatever the theoretical approach to history, the historian has the freedom to organize research findings in a way best suited to the topic. Most obvious is organization by chronology, but some history topics lend themselves to organization by geography, culture, class, or theme.

- **History depends on primary sources.** Therefore the findings of a research inquiry and the depth of its summary narrative depend on the sources available on a given topic. Topics of the more recent past generally have a more easily discoverable primary source paper trail.

- **History is useful.** We humans find the history of the past to be useful in our own times. We research it and write it in our own times, in our own context. Therefore along the way, long-established "historical facts" may be re-interpreted, though still based on hard evidence and ever-mindful of historical context, to improve our contemporary understanding.

- **We humans are not robots.** The real historian has a deep commitment to the ideal of objectivity. For the real journalist, that commitment is like a public trust. But every individual has likes, dislikes, and opinions – even if their one-and-only bias is a preference for maple-walnut instead of strawberry ice cream. As Elizabeth Shown Mills has eloquently stated: "Bias, ego, ideology, patronage, prejudice, pride, or shame cannot shape our decisions as we appraise our evidence."[1] So although we are human, the commitment to the evidence must prevail.

Historical Writing: Descriptive, Narrative, & Analytical

In conceiving the summary, it is wise to consider the three major forms of historical writing: descriptive, narrative, and analytical. Each form has its strengths and limitations, and in fact most comprehensive history writing incorporates elements from all three forms.[2]

In the pure descriptive model, the writer attempts to recreate for the reader the actual experience of a historical event. In creating the atmospheric context of time, place, and conditions, the historian is not unlike the novelist.

In the pure narrative model, the writer recreates the sense of moment-to-moment time and unfolding drama of a historical event. In addition to the event's chronology, this model more generally weaves in the complexities of a historical event.

In the analytical model, the writer addresses the causes, consequences, and motivations relevant to the historical event. In this model, the historian not only calls upon description and narrative of a particular event, but also includes analysis of background causes and direct causes.

Each model has its drawbacks. The limitation of the narrative model is that merely ordering historical events in chronological sequence does not necessarily indicate or resolve any relationship between them. Historian of history methodology John Tosh believes that the narrative form is inadequate for explaining an inventory of broad-scope parallel causes as they relate to day-to-day events. For addressing such complexities, he favors a more analytical approach to writing history.[3]

The analytical approach, however, has its own shortcomings due to its static nature. "Undiluted analytical history raises its own problems," Tosh writes in *The Pursuit of History: Aims, Methods, and New Directions in the Study of History* (2015). "What it gains in intellectual clarity, it loses in historical immediacy." Ultimately Tosh advocates for a flexible use of both analytical and narrative modes. "The truth is that historians need to write in ways that do justice to both the manifest and the latent, both profound forces and surface events."[4]

Despite Tosh's reservations about narrative, he believes that historical writing entirely devoid of it risks becoming "a shapeless incoherent mess," and that "micro-narrative" is the ideal tool for social historians writing about the lives of individuals and smaller social units previously subject only to broad-view abstract analysis.[5]

Three qualities to be refined. The writing of history, in the view of John Tosh, requires the refinement of three qualities: (1) the mastery of primary sources, a mastery that includes critical evaluation; (2) an experience-born "knowledge of life" which translates to an ability to empathize with the people of the past; and (3) verbal and literary skills that can convey mood, ambiance, and temperament.[6]

On the first quality, the ability to perceive, evaluate, and make sense of relationships and patterns is paramount. On the second quality, the writer's own breadth of life experience and self-awareness build a foundation for the sensitive writing of interpretive history. On the third quality, while the need to parse close arguments with qualifiers tends to bog down a forward-moving narrative, the challenge of combining narrative with analysis, according to Tosh, "is essentially a problem of literary form."[7]

Outline and Organization

History and genealogy researchers are usually motivated writers, but that does not make the blank page at the start of a writing project any less daunting. Fortunately, the previous steps along the way – the research plan, the research execution, the evidence derived from sources, and the interpretation of that evidence – usually suggest the outline and organization of the narrative. A professor that harps on the necessity of an outline will prompt groans from the back of the classroom. But a written outline that organizes the raw material of the narrative makes the work of writing go faster and easier.

Outlines are generally of two types, the topic-based outline, and the sentence-based outline. A third approach may use preliminary "mind-mapping" to help identify the main elements of an outline.

• **The topic-based outline** is the most familiar, and consists of short phrases arranged hierarchically, using roman numerals, capital letters, numbers, and lower-case letters, as shown in the example at right.

• **The sentence-based outline** may organize the material in the same way, but the thoughts are expressed in full sentences instead of short phrases. This approach is useful when the content categories have complex details or multiple interconnected causes and effects.

• **The preliminary "mind-map"** exercise of stream-of-consciousness free-hand jotting-and-connecting of key topics may serve as a useful visual aid in arriving at the more formal and linear textual outline. In this approach, using color-coded sticky notes offers the flexibility of re-ordering your ideas as the outline takes shape.

[On this third approach, your author was recently informed by a co-presenter at a major conference that their wild marker-slashing on the white-board is now called *"thinking mosaically,"* and should replace stodgy, logical, linear thinking. I nodded and silently wondered to myself if I was way ahead of my time in the 1960s when I was thinking *kaleidoscopically*. Your author concedes that mind-mapping, *thinking mosaically*, stream-of-consciousness scribbling, or whatever we choose to call it, can be useful in teasing out ideas at the outline stage. But the mind is an amazingly flexible tool, so don't limit its power and range while following – or recoiling from – fad or fashion.]

The Micro-Historian's Guide to
RESEARCH, EVIDENCE, & CONCLUSIONS — *The Summary Narrative*

Example: A topic-based outline
(Note: In case of any doubt, the dummy text and topic are for illustrative purposes only.)

I. Introduction: "The Flat Earth and Me"
II. Hypothesis of a Flat Earth
   A. First-Person Visual Evidence
      1. Growing Up in Nebraska
         a. Confirmed by Visiting Kansas
      2. Waking Up in the Driveway
   B. Historical Evidence
      1. Cave Drawings
   C. Scientific Analysis
      1. Paper by Professor Irwin Corey
III. Objections & Persecution
   A. Examples of Ridicule
   B. Informed Responses
IV. Conclusion – Restate Hypothesis & Proof
   A. Continued Resistance to Conspiracies

Example: A sentence-based outline

I. Introduce "The Flat Earth and Me."
II. Present the flat earth hypothesis.
   A. Relate my first-person evidence.
      1. Tell a few Nebraska flat earth stories.
         a. Tell a few Kansas flat earth stories.
      2. Report the "on-the-driveway" observations.
   B. Cite the historical evidence.
   C. Report on the scientific analysis.
III. Flat earth proponents face constant persecution.
   A. Enumerate examples of ridicule.
   B. Explain the flat-earther's confident response.
IV. Conclude with a restatement of hypothesis.
   B. Vow to resist round earth conspiracies.

Example: A "mind map" aid

"The Flat Earth and Me"
- Historical Evidence
- Scientific Analysis
- Central Hypothesis
- Objections & Persecution
  - Ridicule
  - Responses
- First-Person Experience
  - Nebraska
  - Kansas
  - Waking up flat on the driveway
- Restate hypothesis & vow to resist round earth conspiracies

A helpful first step in building an outline is the literal step away from the computer. When sitting at the computer keyboard, it is too tempting to plunge into the writing. When you step away from the computer, only the pencil, paper, and brain are needed to jot down the framework of the narrative in its simplest form.

For some individuals, visualizing a public speaking presentation to an imaginary rapt-and-friendly audience is helpful in organizing content for an outline. For some people, talking about something is far easier than writing about it. In addition to aiding the organization of material in an outline, visualizing a public speaking presentation can help bring modulation, emphasis, nuance, gesture, and personality into the writing.

Some practical examples of outlines:

• The outline for *Chauncey Richmond & "The Old Buckbee": The Story of a Banjo, Its Maker, and Its Player*, by R. W. Bacon (2018)[8] is represented in the table of contents. The first outlines, however, were tentative scribbles of indecision. Even though the main subjects of the book were quite clear at the outset of research, there were decisions to be made about organization. Should the family histories go before the business histories? Should Chauncey Richmond (1872-1910), the player, go before John Henry Buckbee (1837-1890), the maker? Or vice-versa? Should the Buckbee banjo restoration be towards the beginning? Or at the end? The goal was to present the material with optimal logical flow, so ultimately the decision was to present thorough context, followed by the chronological presentation of the individuals and their stories.

• Likewise for *The Visitor's Guide to the Weeks Brick House & Gardens*, by R. W. Bacon (2015)[9], the table of contents reflects the organization of its content. Because it is a visitor's guide, the material was presented as it would come into relevance for the visitor, starting, for example, with directions to the house from all points. The outline then proceeds from the general to the specific, i.e. from the bigger-picture local history, to the specific family history, the farmstead, the 1710 house, gardens, conservation land, and nature trails.

• The outline for *A Vaudeville Retrospective* (illustrated lecture, performance, & exhibition) (2008-present)[10] serves as an audience guide to the logical progression that addresses the sequence of their curiosities in real time. The outline is chronological, from an introduction/definition, though growth, evolution, decline, and finally to 21st-century manifestations.

Example: *An outline that became a Table of Contents*
From *Chauncey Richmond & "The Old Buckbee: The Story of a Banjo, Its Maker, and Its Player,* by R. W. Bacon (2018).

Table of Contents

Introduction 5

Acknowledgments. 9

Discovering "The Old Buckbee" 11

Essential Context: A Concise History of the Banjo 15

The J. H. Buckbee Banjo Company 43

    John Henry Buckbee (1837-1890) . . . *Genealogical & Biographical* . . 91

    John Henry Buckbee, Jr. (1867-1943). *Genealogical & Biographical* . 107

Chauncey Richmond (1872-1910) . . . . . . *Genealogical & Biographical* . 117

Chauncey Richmond: Lincoln Park Impresario. 133

New Discoveries …and New Questions. 175

Appendix I: Restoring "The Old Buckbee" 179

Appendix II: Research, Evidence, & Conclusions 189

Bibliography 215

Index 218

About the Author 224

Example: An outline that became a Table of Contents
From *The Visitor's Guide to the Weeks Brick House & Gardens*, by R. W. Bacon (2015).

Table of Contents

Introduction 5

Directions to the Weeks Brick House & Gardens 9

Local History Context:
    Greenland, Portsmouth, and Great Bay 11
    Map: Tide Mill Road & the Town Landing 16
    Time Line: Greenland and the World Beyond 17

Family History Context:
    Leonard Weeks (1633-1707) 19
    Samuel Weeks (1670-1746) 22
    L. & S. Weeks Family Group Sheets .... 18 & 23

The Weeks Family Farmstead (1656-1968) 25
    Geographical Context: Weeks Farmstead Map 24

The Weeks Brick House (1710) 31
    Exterior Self-Guided Architectural Tour 32
    Interior Text & Photographic Tour 40

The Grounds & Gardens 47
    Colonial Herb Garden & Victory Garden Plan...... 46

The Conservation Lands & Trails................... 53
    Nature Trails Map 52

Sources & Bibliography 58

About the Author............................... 59

Weeks Brick House Membership & Support 60

The Micro-Historian's Guide to
RESEARCH, EVIDENCE, & CONCLUSIONS   *The Summary Narrative*

Example: An outline for a research-based presentation
From *A Vaudeville Retrospective* (illustrated lecture, performance, & exhibition), by R. W. Bacon (2008-present).

~ A Vaudeville Retrospective ~

A Vaudeville Retrospective is an illustrated lecture – with digitally-projected graphics and audio/video clips – interspersed with live performance segments by presenter R.W. Bacon in his real-time characterization as *"The Last Living Vaudevillian."*

(1) Introduction: What was Vaudeville? How did it get so BIG?
Vaudeville defined; current misconceptions; survivors to the TV era; a typical show; and Vaudeville theatres, big-time & small-time.

(2) Setting the Scene: 19th Century Beginnings
Early 19th-century circus & variety, the mid-19th-century "concert saloon," and late-19th-century entrepreneurs. Industrialization, urbanization, immigration, technological advances – and a middle-class backlash against aristocratic cultural tastemakers.

(3) The Peak Years: The Growth of an Industry
Competing masterminds, moguls, and monopolists build a nationwide industry: Over 2000 theatres, 2000 miscellaneous venues, 30,000-50,000 performers. Talent aiming to please – tycoons aiming to profit. Vaudeville prospered in tandem with the popular music industry – and the new motion picture business.

(4) People of Vaudeville: The Famous & the Forgotten
Human stories of big-timers and small-timers. Forgotten perhaps, but their influence is with is today, sometimes in unlikely places!

(5) The Decline of Vaudeville: Internal & External Forces
The novelty of sound movies drew audiences from Vaudeville, but it does not tell the whole story – internal forces also played a role. Surprising twists illustrate that things are often not as they seem!

(6) Then What Happened? To people, places, ideas, influences?
The better Vaudevillians moved into nightclub, revue, film, or radio work, while lesser talents moved to "small-time" work or left showbusiness. Post-WWII nightclub variety, 1950s-60s TV variety, and late 20th-century "New Vaudeville."

(7) 21st Century Manifestations – The Spirit Remains
A new amalgam of circus, cabaret, "new burlesque," and the growth of Las Vegas as a show capital provides new venues for today's variety acts. The presentation and "packaging" may have changed, but today's variety performers carry on.

Writing the Summary

No mere handful of paragraphs here can ensure attainment of style, grace, and clarity in the craft of writing. As in mastering any craft, there are no real shortcuts. Start with the right tools, the right habits, the right role models ... and then practice, practice, refine, practice, refine again, and practice more. Therefore this brief section on the craft of writing suggests: (1) the writer's essential toolkit; (2) a selection of digestible guides to clear and concise writing; and (3) guides for the genealogist choosing to follow the formal style of the New England Historic Genealogical Society's *The Register: The Journal of American Genealogy*. These suggestions are followed by this exasperated editor's plea for simple and direct expression. Mindful of the responsibility inherent in history writing, this section concludes with a discussion of language selection, point-of-view, and another rumination on the ideal of objectivity.

• **The writer's toolkit.** The writer's essential toolkit consists of a dictionary, grammar guide, and a stylebook. The preferred dictionary is *Merriam-Webster's Collegiate Dictionary* (11th ed., 2003). The authoritative grammar guide is *The Chicago Guide to Grammar, Usage, and Punctuation*, by Bryan Garner (2016). The authoritative stylebook used by most professional publications is *The Chicago Manual of Style* (17th ed., 2017). Those confined in the straitjacket of academic writing may have to submit to the latest changes in the *MLA Style Manual and Guide to Scholarly Publishing* (8th ed., 2016). For no-nonsense professional journalistic writing, consult *The Associated Press Stylebook & Briefing on Media Law* (50th ed., 2017).

• **Guides to clear and concise writing.** Every writer, from beginner to veteran, will benefit from, and be comforted by, these three classics: *On Writing Well: The Classic Guide to Writing Nonfiction* (7th ed., 2006), by William Zinsser; *The Associated Press Guide to News Writing* (3rd ed., 1999), by Rene J. Cappon; and *The Elements of Style* (4th ed., 2000), by William Strunk, Jr. and E. B. White.

• **Guides to NEHGS Register style.** For writers preparing articles for publication in genealogical journals like the *Register* of the New England Historic Genealogical Society, the best guides are from the source, published by NEHGS: *Genealogical Writing in the 21st Century* (2006), edited by Michael J. Leclerc and Henry B. Hoff; and *Guide to Genealogical Writing* (2014), by Penelope L. Stratton and Henry B. Hoff. For guidance on other numbering systems, consult *Numbering Your Genealogy: Basic Systems, Complex Families, and International Kin* (rev. 2008), by Joan F. Curran, Madilyn Coen Crane, and John H. Wray.

The Micro-Historian's Guide to
RESEARCH, EVIDENCE, & CONCLUSIONS   *The Summary Narrative*

- **The exasperated editor's plea** [... adapted from *The Cranky Editor's Book of Intolerable Fox Paws (Oops! Faux Pas!): Helpful Writing & Style Tips So You Won't Look Stoopid*, by Reginald W. Bacon (2014)[11]]. The purpose of writing anything is to communicate, therefore first consider the perspective and interest of the reading audience on the receiving end. Then banish wimpy words and clumsy sentences. Lose the flab, cut the cliches, and drop the jargon. Emulate concise writers. Don't be a bore. Let the reader know you are alive. Look stuff up – so you don't make grade-school usage and spelling errors. Avoid ambiguity. Make sure you make sense. Punctuate attentively. Learn what a "stylebook" is, and then use it. Commit to the craft.

Speaking of language: More thoughts on striving for the ideal of objectivity. At present, history writing is more diverse than ever, as historians, both macro and micro, use a variety of theoretical approaches, types of analysis, and literary models to explore an ever-widening variety of topics. This diversity is a result not only of the global conflicts and social/political shifts of the 20th century, but improvements in educational opportunity and the democratization of information made possible by technological advances. Formerly well-defined boundaries in the social science disciplines are open for passage, and the hope is that researchers, readers, and society-at-large benefit from all the information-sharing and collaboration.

But with all the new freedom in doing history comes a responsibility to the craft. Scholarly objectivity remains paramount, not only in research and evaluation of evidence, but also in writing the summary narrative. This does not mean the writer should not advance a point-of-view based on evidence-based conclusions, but it does mean that the writer should develop and maintain a sharpened awareness of the limits of historical knowledge. This includes an awareness of the point-of-view, phrasing, and even choice of words, as they may betray a bias of which the writer is unaware.

As stated in different ways on previous pages, the attainment of pure-and-perfect objectivity may not be humanly possible. Every writer of history, whether a hifalutin academic or a barely-literate blogger, is a human being first. Every practitioner brings different skills and abilities to a project, but perhaps more significantly, they bring their own world view shaped by life experiences. And everyone's perception of their life experiences is influenced by variables like class, race, ethnicity, gender, family life, culture, language, education, values, ideology, religion, and more. A valuable quality for the history practitioner writing a summary narrative is a self-awareness of one's own biases – the attributes as well as the deficiencies of life experiences. Awareness of biases is the first step to rooting them out, in case they crept in via the unconscious nuance of the writer's verbiage.[12]

So, just because perfect objectivity may be impossible to attain, we imperfect humans can still strive for the ideal and write informative and useful history to share with our fellow beings. Make sure your verbiage says what you mean to say, in the tone in which you mean to say it. When you are satisfied, then it's time to "polish the jewel" with editing and proofreading.

Editing & Proofreading

Editing. A narrative in its close-to-finished state needs test readers and, ideally, at least one real editor. There are different types of readers, as well as multiple kinds of editors.

Engage test readers that are well-versed in the subject matter of the narrative, along with test readers that are literate, interested non-specialists. At best, the specialist readers will identify points of fact that need clarification; and the non-specialist readers will identify places that require more explanation or better transitions. The specialists and non-specialists, although not professional editors, will also likely notice the most obvious misspellings or typographical errors.

A truism is that every writer needs some kind of editorial scrubbing – even if that writer is an editor. For large projects like books, editing is broken down into phases: concept development; content and organization; grammar and usage; fact-checking; and copy editing. Some editors specialize, and some editors do it all. In a do-it-yourself microhistory research project, the researcher-writer may be tempted to do their own editing. The advice here is to at least engage professional copy editing, the category that concerns the application of consistent and proper capitalization, punctuation, spelling, and typographic style. Note that while your test readers may be very astute and worthy individuals who are kind to children and small animals, most likely they are not real editors. Nor is your kindly Aunt Tillie, the retired English teacher. Nor is your favorite niece who always scores 100% on her 8th-grade spelling text. If you are serious about your work, engage a *real* professional editor. A real editor will save the non-professional writer from embarrassment in print.

Most of us know that sometimes the budget overrules good sense. For the microhistorian with a micro-bank balance who elects not to hire an editor: A remarkably helpful self-editing exercise is reading your own writing aloud. In the process, you may discover sentence constructions that seem perfectly fine on paper, but just "don't sound right." The reading aloud test is especially useful in rooting out clumsy phrasing, ambiguities, and punctuation oversights.

Proofreading. Note that the all-important proofreading function is different from copy editing. Ideally, copy editing is for sense, structure, punctuation, spelling, and usage, while proofreading is for catching typos and double-checking typographic stylebook consistency. Edit first; proofread last. Do not rely entirely on a spell-check application, because, though helpful for obvious errors, ultimately spell-check applications are dumb. For example, in a grateful missive to your favorite professor, a spell-check application will never detect "Dead Professor Jones:" in the salutation. And if a typographic error does make it through in your printed and published work, go ahead and beat yourself up over it, but don't go for a lights-out knockout to the canvas. It is a fact that most books, even those from the "Big-Five" publishers, have a few undetected typographical errors in the first printing. Just make sure to fix everything for the next printing.

Footnotes and endnotes. Setting the standard for decades, now in its 17th edition, is the previously-mentioned *Chicago Manual of Style*. The most comprehensive treatment of the subject at present, however, for both historical and genealogical projects, is *Evidence Explained: Citing History Sources from Artifacts to Cyberspace* (2007), by Elizabeth Shown Mills. The subject is addressed in greater detail, with examples, in Appendix III: Source Citation 101.

Summary Narratives: Practical Examples and Issues

• **This writer's agony.** Although this writer's agony is generally not apparent to the reader, the majority of the sentences in all of my books were twisted inside-out, flipped backwards, wrestled with, and recast several times before reaching a satisfactory state. This approach is business-as-usual for most writers. Even if the rough draft flows along briskly, the relentless paring and re-shaping is an integral part of the craft that leads to the finished product.

• **Where is the thrill?** In *Chauncey Richmond & "The Old Buckbee: The Story of a Banjo, Its Maker, and Its Player* (2018)[13], the narratives about Chauncey Richmond and John Henry Buckbee are packed with comparatively dry information about local geography, census records, and real estate transactions. But in the absence of more

The Micro-Historian's Guide to
RESEARCH, EVIDENCE, & CONCLUSIONS   *The Summary Narrative*

thrilling stories of wild adventures – or even mundane routines – there was a concentrated effort to give the paragraph-to-paragraph transitions enough motive power to sustain the chronological narrative. Whether the effort was successful is a verdict up to the reader. For the historian or genealogist, as long as the narrative remains absolutely faithful to the evidence, it is never a crime to keep the reader awake.

- **Author participation in the narrative.** In 2008 your author was engaged by the New England Park Association to prepare a historical overview of the turn-of-the-20th-century trolley-park era in the region for the organization's publication, the *NEPA Exchange*.[14] The resulting article employed two distinguishing characteristics of microhistory: (1) an exploration of the popular culture of "ordinary people," and (2) author participation in the narrative.

A bit of context: In the 1880s, electrified transit systems replaced horse-drawn trolleys in cities large and small. The trolley companies, seeking maximum profit – and frustrated by paying a flat monthly fee for electricity – explored every opportunity to increase ridership. One solution was to create a destination that would induce entire families to ride the trolley – and pay the fare – on Saturdays, Sundays, and evenings. The brilliant idea for such a destination was the company-owned park. The dozens of parks that sprung up throughout New England were usually situated at the end of the trolley line. Some began as no more than a picnic grove and gazebo, but by the early 20th century, many evolved to include a dizzying array of arcade games, restaurants, dance halls, vaudeville shows, thrill rides, swimming, and diving donkeys. The automobile that revolutionized American life brought an end to trolley transportation, but many of the parks endured for decades before eventual closure. Some still survive as amusement parks, such as Canobie Lake Park (N.H.), Quassy Park (Conn.), and Riverside Park (now Six Flags New England; Mass.).

Author participation in the narrative was a significant component of the article, as during a long performance career, I "tread the boards" on the well-worn stages of many parks during their last gasps of existence. Often the theatrical agents that engaged us had procured entertainment for the parks since the 1920s, such as at the now-defunct Lincoln Park, Mountain Park, and Whalom Park (all in Mass.); and Rocky Point (R.I.). While surrounded by the crumbling ornamentation of the outdoor theatres, I soaked up detail from conversations with folks whose families had attended the parks for generations. In the resulting article, reportage of my first-person experience added depth to the more conventionally accumulated historical evidence.

The Micro-Historian's Guide to
RESEARCH, EVIDENCE, & CONCLUSIONS   *The Summary Narrative*

- **What? No murder?** In 2011 your author completed a drawn-out research project that culminated in publication of *A Micro-History of the Tannersville Four-Corners*[15]. The research was narrowly focused on the evolution of a crossroads in a small town in the northern High Peaks region of New York's Catskill Mountains. The crossroads that began with a tavern for seasonal bark-peelers and leather-tanners in the late 18th century grew to be the center of a cluster of Victorian-era grand and not-so-grand hotels for vacationing New Yorkers by the late 19th century. The next hundred years after that brought even more changes. The book chronicled the economic and social history, the changes in property ownership and use, and the waves of different ethnic groups that influenced the course of the town's history.

The reason this project took extra years to complete was a delay that began with an encounter with a property owner near the Four-Corners area of study who had a different view of what constitutes history. This house and property in the study area had at various times been a newspaper office, a print shop, a newsstand, a candy shop, and a feed store. Sandwiched between two Victorian-era hotels built during the boom years in the 1880s, it was once also directly across the street from a livery stable and blacksmith shop – which gave way to a gas station in the early days of the automobile. In the late 1930s the structure was converted into a combination residence and headquarters for a New York-to-the-Catskills limousine service. A summer lodging house was also built on a hill behind the residence.

At first the relatively new owner of the unpretentious residence was welcoming, but a year later, upon seeing photographs of the house taken from across the public street, from a public sidewalk, a deep paranoia set in. Eventually the worry was expressed that from the photos and maps planned for the book, unidentified miscreants in town could determine the location of doors, windows, and mailbox. Despite all the charm and calming assurances I could summon to the cause of research and history, the response was "This house isn't historic! No one was ever murdered here!"

I took the high road. I did not want to be the first victim. People are entitled to feel how they want to feel. It takes all kinds to make up this world of ours. Even though I was secure in photographer's rights and publisher's rights, the owner's thinly-veiled threat of a nuisance lawsuit was motivation enough to re-crop certain photos and tiptoe around some recent history. The historic maps remained, and the gist of the content was not compromised. Relating this experience serves as a caution that some people hold different conceptions of history.

- **The "Case" of the Banjo-Mandolin.** In 2015 your author's purchase of a c. 1920 no-name banjo-mandolin on Ebay and the research that ensued culminated in a microhistory narrative that dovetailed with the macrohistory of early-20th-century jazz and the popular music of the "Roaring 20s." The two-part series entitled "The 'Case' of the Banjo-Mandolin," which appeared in *Variety Arts Gazette* (2016-2017)[16], detailed the course and outcome of research that was prompted by the discovery of a tiny pen-scratched name-and-address on the inside flap of the beat-up original instrument case.

Cross-referenced research of census, immigration, college, and business records determined that "Sam Clearfield" (1903-1989) of 809-811 South Street in Philadelphia, Pa. was the first American-born son of dry-goods store proprietor Isaac "Ike" Klarfeld and his wife, Pearl, who arrived in the U.S. from Russia in 1900. As a young pharmacy student at Temple University, Sam Clearfield was one of many thousands of college-age banjo, mandolin, and uke strummers across the U.S. who played the jazz-inflected soundtrack of the decade. He is a perfect anonymous everyman example – in contrast to the big names – of the children of Russian Jewish immigrants who contributed to popular culture in the early 20th-century, helping to shape American jazz, popular music, and showbusiness. There are plenty of well-known examples: songwriters Irving Berlin (1888-1989), Jerome Kern (1885-1945), George (1898-1937) & Ira (1896-1983) Gershwin, and Harold Arlen (1905-1986); vaudevillians and proto-jazz singers Al Jolson (1886-1950), Sophie Tucker (1884-1966), Eddie Cantor (1892-1964); and swing era bandleader and clarinet virtuoso Benny Goodman (1909-1986). [For more about the convergence of African-American jazz, New York Tin-Pan-Alley pop, klezmer, showbiz, and Jewishness, consult *Funny, It Doesn't Sound Jewish: How Yiddish Songs and Synagogue Melodies Influenced Tin Pan Alley, Broadway, & Hollywood*, by Jack Gottlieb (2004); *America's Songs: The Stories Behind the Songs of Broadway, Hollywood, & Tin Pan Alley*, by Michael Lasser (2006, 2013); and *Jazz Age Jews* by Michael Alexander (2003).]

Sam Clearfield graduated from Temple University in 1927 and enjoyed a long career as a pharmacist. His son became a surgeon – and an amateur violinist and chamber music aficionado. Sam's granddaughter is the musicologist and composer Andrea Clearfield. When she learned that a historian and musicologist-without-portfolio was in possession of her grandfather's banjo-mandolin, which was long out of the family, she was glad to know that it was in good hands, and glad to know that fellow researchers as well as future audiences might benefit from the micro-to-macro interpretations.

The Micro-Historian's Guide to
RESEARCH, EVIDENCE, & CONCLUSIONS *The Summary Narrative*

- **A microhistory narrative that touches all the bases.** Just as this volume on research planning and execution was nearing completion, an exemplary microhistory narrative was published that is at once notable and instructive: *A Newburyport Marine in World War I: The Life and Legacy of Eben Bradbury* (2018)[17], by Bethany Groff Dorau. In your author's view, this book hits the microhistory jackpot, checking off, between its covers, all the major principles of the genre.

The narrative begins with an introduction to one extended family through several generations, then narrows the focus to one family line in the singular town of Newburyport, Mass., then narrows the focus even more to the subject individual, Eben Bradbury (1897-1918), and his family. The narrative details Eben's youth, budding adulthood, and his service in the U.S. Marines in WWI that ended with his death in the fiery battles at Belleau Wood in France on June 12, 1918. To be sure, no battle death should be ordinary, but in this case the aftermath – the bureaucratic stumbles that delayed notification of the family about Eben's death for four long months – became especially extraordinary.

The narrative then details the family's move to California after Eben's death, where Eben's parents lived out their years. But that is just the beginning of discoveries on both sides of the Atlantic in which the author connects to the macrohistory and is a key actor in the narrative.

The author began with a story untold, just a name and death date on a plaque on a rock in Eben's hometown, an obscure memorial isolated by automobile traffic. Pursuit of this story eventually led the author to Belleau Wood in France, site of the battle carnage, and the Aisne-Marne American Cemetery where Eben Bradbury is interred.

The story of how the book came to be is one that is full of chance encounters, happy coincidence, and truth-is-stranger-than-fiction serendipity. The story could not have come together as it did without the separate discovery and return to Newburyport of *two* troves of family letters, discarded bundles saved for no particular reason by a couple of California antiques collectors. How the bundles of family letters found their way to the author is part of the research narrative.

Was this luck? Could be. But the author, a longtime museum/history professional who earned a master's degree in history, had years of preparation to maximize her chances to be lucky. She was steeped in context. She grew up in Eben Bradbury's town, and as a teenager she hung out near the site of the family's old drug store. As a young museum professional she wrote an authoritative history of the town's first 150 years. As a more seasoned historian she wrote chapters for

The Micro-Historian's Guide to
RESEARCH, EVIDENCE, & CONCLUSIONS   *The Summary Narrative*

textbooks on World War I – including content on the battle at Belleau Wood. So, were her discoveries mere happenstance? As gnarly old football coaches like to grunt after a savvy veteran makes a "lucky" play to win a game in the final seconds, "It was all due to experience, preparation, and conditioning. You make your own luck."

When you are prepared with a foundation of method and context, you can better recognize "luck" coming your way, and you will be equipped to take advantage of it. This is not unlike the role of preparation in "making your own luck" in the search for an ideal job, home, or mate. Your project may not yield a book, but when you follow procedure, research comprehensively – *and* make room for serendipity – you could "get lucky" with raw material for a sparkling narrative.

NOTES to The Summary Narrative

(1) Elizabeth Shown Mills. *Evidence Explained: Citing History Sources from Artifacts to Cyberspace* (3rd ed.). (Baltimore, Md.: Genealogical Publishing Co., 2017), pg. 15.

(2) John Tosh. *The Pursuit of History: Aims, Methods, and New Directions in the Study of History* (6th ed.). (New York, N.Y.: Routledge, 2015), pg. 122-147.

(3) Ibid., pg. 128.

(4) Ibid., pg. 131.

(5) Ibid., pg. 132.

(6) Ibid., pg. 142.

(7) Ibid., pg. 144.

(8) R. W. Bacon. *Chauncey Richmond and "The Old Buckbee": The Story of a Banjo, Its Maker, and Its Player*. (Newburyport, Mass.: Variety Arts Press, 2018).

(9) R. W. Bacon. *The Visitor's Guide to the Weeks Brick House & Gardens*. (Newburyport, Mass.: Variety Arts Press, 2015).

(10) R. W. Bacon. *A Vaudeville Retrospective* (illustrated lecture, performance, & exhibition), 2008-present. (*www.VarietyArtsEnterprises.com*)

(11) R. W. Bacon. *The Cranky Editor's Book of Intolerable Fox Paws (Oops! Faux Pas!)*. (Newburyport, Mass.: Variety Arts Press, 2014).

(12) Martha Howell & John Prevenier. *From Reliable Sources: An Introduction to Historical Methods*. (Ithaca, N.Y.: Cornell University Press, 2001), pg. 143-148.

(13) Bacon, *Chauncey Richmond and "The Old Buckbee": The Story of a Banjo, Its Maker, and Its Player*.

(14) R. W. Bacon. "Historian of early 20th-century entertainment tells the story of the New England 'trolley park'," *NEPA Exchange*, Summer 2008. (Manchester, Conn.: New England Park Association, 2008).

(15) R. W. Bacon. *A Micro-History of the Tannersville Four-Corners*. (Newburyport, Mass.: Variety Arts Press, 2008, 2011).

(16) R. W. Bacon. "The 'Case' of the Banjo Mandolin," *Variety Arts Gazette*, Winter 2016, Winter 2017. (Newburyport, Mass.: Variety Arts Press, 2016, 2017).

(17) Bethany Groff Dorau. *A Newburyport Marine in World War I: The Life and Legacy of Eben Bradbury*. (Charleston, S.C.: The History Press, 2018).

Parting Thoughts – Timeless & Timely

These parting thoughts on research, evidence, and conclusions are a catch-all of observations, tips, warnings, and exhortations deemed valuable enough to stand tall at this terminus. At first the intent was to present a few tidbits to reinforce the principles advanced in the book. Current circumstances, however – i.e. a free press under attack, the disequilibrium of fact, the denigration of truth-seeking scholarship, and a national crisis of media literacy – suggest that the *timeless* principles of research, evidence, and conclusions may be more *timely* than ever. For those moved to aid the cause of media literacy, visit the Center for Media Literacy (*www.medialit.org*) to learn how its core concepts dovetail with principles of evidence analysis. For those hungry for the tidbits, digest the following parting thoughts:

- **Evidence can be more than just text.** It took a shelf-life of 50 years for the mustachioed "Cap'n Crunch" on the cereal box to be revealed as a mere "Commander." A sharp-eyed, detail-oriented observer noticed that the 1963 cartoon creation had only the three gold stripes of a naval commander on his sleeve instead of a captain's four. Keep a sharp eye out for obvious and not-so-obvious evidence in photos, illustrations, ephemera, video, and all visual sources.

- **"So what?" and "Who cares?"** Make sure your research project answers these questions for both you and your readers. When you answer these questions, your project may yield the ultimate complimentary reader comment: "I never knew that (… fill in the blank …)!"

- **Interpretation … or not?** This book has melded the research approaches of the investigative journalist, the historian, and the genealogist. To be clear, in real news journalism, it's "just the facts, ma'am," with no interpretation beyond sorting out the priority of the "who, what, when, where, and why." Conversely, in the history field, interpretation is a component of the historian's job. The genealogy field stands somewhat apart, with its proof standards and report formats.

- **Don't even think of it.** Of course the following phrases will not turn up in your work of genealogy to introduce fanciful claims: "It is said that ... ," "Tradition holds that ... ," and "It has long been known that ...." Folklore and mythology can be entertaining and even instructive, but it is not fact. Beware of balancing your assemblage of laboriously acquired evidence on somebody else's jumble of lazy assumptions.

• **No baloney.** As above, don't take a tiny grain of truth and try to make a whole loaf of baloney.

• **Calibrate your baloney detector.** Speaking of baloney, among the most valuable professional tools of an investigative journalist is an up-to-date and well-calibrated "baloney detector." This tool, refined through experience, is usually called by its more crude name. A good "baloney detector" is also useful to the history and genealogy researcher faced with rooting out fact from myth in richly embellished writings of the past. Keep your detector handy.

• **Nothing is really something.** What is not discovered during exhaustive investigations can be just as significant as what is found. The absence of evidence is itself evidence: The evidence of absence. (N.B.: This is not a loophole excuse for half-baked research efforts.)

• **Let 'em know how you know.** Bring the reader into your world. Share with the reader the process of your research and the excitement of your discoveries. Enthusiasm is usually contagious, so your reader is likely to be more engaged.

• **Show some spark.** It really is possible to lay out bone-dry evidence and still confirm to the reader, through your verbiage, that you have a pulse and are indeed among the living. Let the spark of enthusiasm for your subject show in your writing.

• **A community of understanding.** When your research project concludes with a cogent summary narrative to disseminate, your readers, though perhaps anonymous to each other, form a new community of shared understanding.

• **Your work is not a lark. It's making your mark.** Your research efforts may seem fun and fleeting now, yielding discoveries of limited interest. But consider that your research and summary may have a long life. Make your work timeless as well as timely. Keep in mind that your work could become a source for generations not yet born.

• **Check it out.** Finally, worth repeating here is the apocryphal story of the long-ago cigar-chomping newspaper editor who, in teaching a cub reporter a lesson on the imperative of fact-checking, admonished his young charge: "Yer mother sez she loves ya'? So what?! You still gotta check it out!"

Appendix I: Local History 101

This brief introduction to local history – its rationale, background, resources, and tools – quickly defers to three foundational books, and then makes way for the author's essay adapted from *Just a Tot in Tannersville*, and *A Micro-History of the Tannersville Four-Corners* (2011).

The rationale for local history. Local history encompasses the study of individuals, families, neighborhoods, communities, businesses, farms, schools, churches, institutions, organizations, built environments, and all subjects related to the everyday life of ordinary people. Just as in broader-scope history, it may also include social, political, economic, and environmental history. The social benefits of rigorously executed local history include discovering causes of present circumstances, correcting skewed public memory, and exposing myths. Research in local history can reveal the origin of conditions, causes of change, and links to broader history. Local history studies expand context, enhance perspective, and ideally, facilitate understanding.

Local history then and now. As practiced today, local history is a relatively new offshoot of the "new social history." In the 19th century, local histories in the U.S. evolved from early post-Revolutionary War myth-making ... to Colonial Revival myth-making late in the century. Today's local historians still contend with the deficiencies of late-19th-century local histories that created an idealized past and elevated early-settler forbears to near-sainthood. For most of the 20th century, academic historians seeking essential truths about important issues did not want to be contaminated by association with amateurs seeking only picayune details of local life. Helping to elevate local history was the formation in 1940 of the American Association for State & Local History (*www.aaslh.org*). Today the embracing of the new microhistory by academia lends legitimacy to local history.

The resources of local history. Resources include documents, public records, photos, recordings, material objects, buildings, landscapes, and more. There is more to history than documents in a library. And be aware that *everything* cannot be found on the internet.

The Micro-Historian's Guide to
RESEARCH, EVIDENCE, & CONCLUSIONS   *Appendix I: Local History 101*

The local historian's toolkit. The aspiring local historian must understand the usefulness and importance of unbiased local history to one's fellow citizens, now and in the future. One must appreciate the range of topics; learn to dig for answers to the "who, what, when, where, and why" questions; and learn to evaluate evidence. More concrete tools are the mastery of census research and source citation. And let's not forget the all-important baloney detector (pg. 92).

Build a foundation of knowledge. Highly recommended for theory, practice, and rumination are *Nearby History: Exploring the Past Around You* (2010), by David E. Kyvig and Myron A. Marty; *On Doing Local History* (2014), by Carol Kammen; and *A Place to Remember: Using History to Build Community* (1999), by Robert R. Archibald. Build a firm foundation by soaking up the wisdom in these volumes.

[The following essay is adapted from *Just a Tot in Tannersville, and A Micro-History of the Tannersville Four-Corners* (2011), your author's personal memoir and local history of the brief post-WWII Armenian resort boom in a small town in New York's Catskill Mountains. The essay is food-for-thought for local historians navigating the foggy intersection of rigorous local history and rosy personal nostalgia.]

An Essay of Interest to Local Historians

One concern addressed in the introduction *Just a Tot in Tannersville* and *A Micro-History of the Tannersville Four-Corners* was the intersection of personal memoir and local history. This intersection has long been of interest, first from the point of view of a historian of early-20th-century popular entertainment, and then from the point of view of a museum professional interpreting historic properties. While writing the books and navigating the intersection, I recorded observations that may be useful to others considering similar local history projects, and who may have their own foggy intersections ahead.

Over the course of a long career as a performing artist, I read widely on the history of early-20th-century vaudeville and the roots of my on-stage specialties. Most easily accessible were the fawning showbiz biographies and factually-suspect autobiographies of the stars. Before showbusiness, I was a journalist and editor, so I regarded this reading as required dues-paying. Once I read all that fluff, I moved on to first-person accounts of non-performing agents, entrepreneurs, managers, and journalists. Then I digested scholarly works on vaudeville, written by academics removed from the time, place, and vocation. My next

The Micro-Historian's Guide to
RESEARCH, EVIDENCE, & CONCLUSIONS   *Appendix I: Local History 101*

category of reading included newspapers, magazines, letters, theatre programs, and trade publications. The years of reading and research opened my eyes to the brazen embellishments, careful whitewashing, and innocent misinformation of first-person accounts. So by the time I was immersed in theory as a graduate student in museum studies, I was sensitized to that intersection where nostalgia and fact collide.

"Outsider" & "Insider" local historians. My work in the museum field – and residence in a New England town with beginnings in 1635 – means that sensitivity to local history is imperative. Descendants of early-settler families still reside locally, and have a valid claim to a share of local history. Since I am a non-native "outsider," if I detect that my history work might challenge earlier interpretations, it is essential that I be mindful of the "insider" local historians. Gentle handling is required when separating their valuable knowledge and insight from what may be long-held myths, personal nostalgia, family grudges, or political agendas. In my view, for local history projects, every word of a community's most sage citizens should be preserved. But when it comes to checking facts, verifying sources, researching context, laying out big-picture perspective, and writing interpretive history, an impartial outsider, whether professional or ardent amateur, might have a better chance at achieving an objective, fact-based end-result.

In writing *Just a Tot in Tannersville*, and *A Micro-History of the Tannersville Four-Corners*, I was both "insider" and "outsider." I was an "insider" when I wrote my personal memories of 1950s Tannersville. I was an "outsider" when I compiled and interpreted the early history of the town and made subjective observations of the town today.

Personal recollections. I gave plenty of thought to handling personal recollections. Yet I did not want to over-think them. Intellectually I knew that my memories were from when I was just a naive kid. But youthful memories do have a purity and legitimacy of their own. Rather than recast my memories from a mature point of view, my aim was to leave them intact. I decided that the vocabulary could be adult, but the thoughts should be those of a kid. The grown-up attitudes and any so-called wisdom of maturity could be added later. What I tried to avoid was the intrusion of overly-sweet nostalgia.

Nostalgia: "The soft-porn of memory"? In youthful memoirs, I know how easy it is to allow nostalgia to slip in. The same goes for myth, folklore, and misconceptions. Sam Allis, a one-time columnist for *The Boston Globe*, referred to nostalgia as "the soft-porn of memory," an apt description. Every town seems to have its vocal champion of the "good old days," and they are usually supporters of local history

The Micro-Historian's Guide to
RESEARCH, EVIDENCE, & CONCLUSIONS   *Appendix I: Local History 101*

projects. When I worked as a journalist and conducted hundreds of interviews for newspaper and magazine features, it became clear to me that it is perfectly normal for people, even those who experienced hardships early in life, to romanticize or idealize their youth. A coordinator of a local history project would do well to encourage the passion of "good old days" contributors, but also be vigilant to identify myth, folklore, misconceptions, and nostalgia for what they are.

"What happened in Tannersville?" When I was in elementary school in Arlington, Mass., my school was on Paul Revere Road. This was the road that Paul Revere supposedly galloped by on during his famous ride of 1776, so the local connection made all of us kids perk up for our history lessons. So when I visited other places I would wonder "What went on here?" In Tannersville in the mid-1950s, there were a lot of dilapidated, haunted-looking, old Victorian-era hotels, some abandoned. "Why?" I wondered. "What is this all about?" The stores on Main Street were trimmed with late-Victorian decorative frou-frou. Many stores had false facades, like a cheap Wild West boomtown. "Something went on here," I thought, but I was not sure what it was. Meanwhile, I was consumed by the present: Helping out at my grandmother's small lodging house sandwiched between two formerly "grand" hotels, people-watching on the crowded sidewalks, and listening to exotic Armenian music wafting from the belly-dance club far into the night. There were many summers of non-stop bustling activity that I, with my puny one decade of life experience, believed defined the town's past and would go on forever into the future.

Things are not always as they seem. My curiosity never waned about Tannersville. Through the years I learned its history incrementally. Although I was a wide-eyed witness to mid-20th-century history, things were not always as they seemed. Here are a just a few examples:

• **Rip Van Winkle Lake.** As a boy I figured the lake was just as prehistoric as the rest of the mountain geography. Then a few years ago I read a 1911 newspaper article about plans for a man-made lake in Tannersville to be formed from a wide spot in Meadow Brook Creek.

• **The Armenian summer population.** When I was a boy, I was curious about Armenian music, food, and culture. The music was lively. The food aromas were intoxicating. The people seemed happy and animated. I looked for Armenia on my globe, but could not find it. My father told me it was "part of Russia," i.e. the Soviet Union at that time, but it was years before I could find it on a map. And it was years after that before I learned of the 1915-1924 genocide, the not-so-happy reason why many Armenians fled their homeland in the first place.

The Micro-Historian's Guide to
RESEARCH, EVIDENCE, & CONCLUSIONS   *Appendix I: Local History 101*

- **Onteora Park & Elka Park.** When I was a boy all I knew was that residents of Onteora Park and Elka Park provided steady business for my grandfather's limousine service to-and-from New York City. Decades later I learned that the genesis of these exclusive enclaves about 1890 was a reaction to the growing clientele of Jewish people in area hotels. The wealthy could afford to escape the crowding of the middle class, and the motive was a not-so-thinly-disguised anti-Semitism.

- *The King & I* **at the Orpheum.** In the summer of 1956 I watched Yul Brynner's "King" and Deborah Kerr's "Anna" whirl around in "Shall We Dance" a dozen times on the screen of Tannersville's moviehouse, the Orpheum. Then I grew up and learned that it was Gertrude Lawrence who made the role of Anna famous on stage, but died during the run in 1952. Then I learned that it was not Deborah Kerr, but Marni Nixon who performed the songs in the movie. Then I learned that 21-year-old Marni Nixon had a device placed in her microphone to deepen her voice and reduce its youthful ring. What next? Then I learned that the macho Yul Brynner, a chain smoker, was so out-of-breath between takes of "Shall We Dance" that he had to take oxygen. (Things are often not what they seem, especially in the movies.)

So ... is first-person history reliable? These are only a few of the examples in the original essay, but they illustrate how off-base the local historian could be if relying only on first-person on-the-scene reports as irrefutable "truth." The reality was that Tannersville's post-WWII Armenian resort boom that briefly revitalized the one-time Victorian-era summer destination lasted only 20 years. Then the sagging, vacant hotels were lost, one-by-one, to a puzzling rash of "lightning fires."

There is no knowledge without context; no understanding without perspective. In *Just a Tot in Tannersville*, much of the content consists of my subjective memories of youth. When deep into the project, I came to believe that my own wrestling with the narrow perspective of my youthful observations from the porch on Railroad Avenue has much in common with the challenges faced by other local historians who write from the narrow perspective of their own *figurative* "front porch." Granted, most local historians are not naive kids, but the analogy is useful. In the 1950s, I saw and knew everything from the "observation deck" of my grandmother's front porch. Who is to say my take on history isn't so? I was there and saw everything! But of course my context and perspective were almost nonexistent. Therefore be mindful that in local history, global history, or even daily life, there is no *knowledge* without *context*; no *understanding* without *perspective*. **– R.W. Bacon (2011)**

The Micro-Historian's Guide to
RESEARCH, EVIDENCE, & CONCLUSIONS   Appendix I: Local History 101

For local historians & genealogists: The mastery of census research skills is essential

Federal census enumeration of United States citizens has taken place every decade since 1790.

It is important to note that:

- The census format and the information gathered changed almost every decade.

- Before 1850, only heads-of-household were named (usually male), with other household members tallied by age group.

- Beginning in the 1850 census, all household members were recorded by name. Information gathered included age, occupation, and state or country of birth.

- Information gathered in later census years included many other changing categories.

- Note that not every individual in the U.S. was enumerated in every census. Those in traveling professions often were on the move during enumeration periods.

- Note that 99.99% of the 1890 census was lost in a fire in 1921.

The National Archives and Records Administration (*https://www.archives.gov/research/genealogy/charts-forms*) offers downloadable blank census forms customized for each decade that are ideal for making readable transcriptions of original less-than-perfect census images.

Appendix II: Genealogy 101

This breezy Genealogy 101 introduction is condensed from the author's guide of the same name prepared for family history programs at historic house museums and family farmsteads in New England. Additional resources are listed in the bibliography (pg. 105).

How do I get started? If you are reading this, chances are you have some familiarity with the process of family history research. If you are a veteran researcher, you can skip to the last section: "How do I finish?" If you are just starting your quest, this introduction is for you.

"Start with yourself": A truism in genealogy. This truism can be extended to "start with what you know." By recording information you know with certainty about yourself, your parents, and grandparents, you are creating a template for every individual you research in the future. Make copies of family birth certificates, marriage licenses, and death certificates to document your known facts. (This brings to mind another truism: "Genealogy without proof is mythology.")

Consult your older family members not only for facts and documentation, but also for anecdotes, photos, obituaries, memorabilia, hints, and clues about the lives and locations of earlier generations. Make sure to record details of even the flimsy family tales. After all, in your future research, you may be the one who finds evidence to confirm or debunk family folklore. Write or visit the towns of family birth, marriage, and death events to obtain copies of vital records. (For information on how to do this, consult the books listed in the bibliography.)

Organize your information. After collecting information on several generations, get the information onto family group sheets (pg. 101) and pedigree charts (pg. 102). Remember, five generations yields yourself and 30 ancestors. Ten generations? Yourself and 1023 ancestors. Genealogy software can generate charts from your data.

Assemble your "genealogist's toolkit." You may not aspire to be a professional genealogist, but you can still use professional tools, like *Professional Genealogy* and *Evidence Explained* by Elizabeth Shown

Mills; and *The Source: A Guidebook of American Genealogy* by Loretto Dennis Szucs and Sandra Hargraves Luebking (eds.).

Don't forget historical context. As you extend your collection of ancestors back in time, remember that family history is more than a collection of names and dates. As you explore sources you will find information about occupations, military service, family migrations, etc. Further research into the local geography, local history, and social history will enhance your understanding of your ancestors in their time. Just make sure to keep your baloney detector handy (*see pg. 94*). With enough research, you will find that true stories about your ancestors are usually more interesting than folklore or fiction.

Don't worry about nuts on the family tree. If you are ambitous enough to identify 12 generations of ancestors (i.e. 4094), you'll find that, if you are truly objective, you'll have among them roughly an equal number of saints and sinners, marvels and misfits, visionaries and dolts – with most clumped in the middle ground of undistinguished but fortunate survivors.

The internet: Information and misinformation. The internet has been a boon to genealogical research, but it has also enabled the spread of misinformation. Today it is easier than ever to search census records, vital records, military records, city directories, newspapers, local histories, ... and *undocumented* family histories. So remember that the principles of research and documentation remain. It is tempting to "piggyback" onto someone else's research. But when consulting research of others, make sure to confirm the documentation yourself.

How do I stay organized? Keep a research log (pg. 29 & 102) for every individual, noting what sources have been explored, what documentation has been found, and the next steps in research for each. A research log can be a simple notebook, or can be "notes" in a genealogy software application. You will find that as you work back in time, vital records are harder to come by. When faced with such an impasse, the resourceful researcher turns to probate, land, or other records from which to interpolate ages and relationships. To stay organized as investigations broaden, a written log aids time efficiency.

OK, now I know how to get started. But how do I finish? At some point in your research, you need to summarize your findings. Undoubtedly your summary will include some unanswered questions, dead ends, or "brick walls." That's why every genealogy project is never truly finished, but instead remains "a work in progress." As one chipper, tireless family history researcher once stated with glee: "Every time you discover a new ancestor, you've got two more to look for!"

Family Group Sheet

HUSBAND

Name: Occupation(s):

	Date	Place	Event	Date/Place/Details
Born			Immigration:	
Died			Naturalization:	
Buried			Military Service:	
Married			Cause of Death:	
Father			Date of Will:	
Mother			Other Marriages:	

WIFE

Birth Name: Occupation(s):

	Date	Place	Event	Date/Place/Details
Born			Immigration:	
Died			Naturalization:	
Buried			Military Service:	
Married			Cause of Death:	
Father			Date of Will:	
Mother			Other Marriages:	

CHILDREN

M/F	Name	Birth Date	Birth Place	Spouse Name & Marriage Date/Place	Death Date & Place

Researching a family: Use a family group sheet

When research involves tracking a family's movement through time and places, a family group sheet, in hard-copy or digital form, is useful to record the basic vital records details of a family unit in one place. The National Archives and Records Administration offers a downloadable blank family group sheet at *https://www.archives.gov/research/genealogy/charts-forms*.

The Micro-Historian's Guide to
RESEARCH, EVIDENCE, & CONCLUSIONS   Appendix II: Genealogy 101

Researching an individual: A sample checklist

Name: _____

Date of Birth: _____ Place of Birth: _____

Date of Death: _____ Place of Death: _____

Family Sources	Town/City Records	State Records	Federal Records
___Relatives	___Birth Record	___Birth Record	___Social Security
___Baby Book	___Marriage Record	___Death Record	___Death Index
___Bible	___Tax Records	___Land Record	___Federal Land Record
___Diary/Journal	___Death Record	___Military Record	___Military Record
___Genealogy	___Cemetery Record	___State History	___Pension Record
___Letters	___Church Record	___State Census	___Ship Passenger List
___Awards	___City Directory		
___Memberships	___Hospital Record	**Printed Sources**	**Federal Census Records**
___Passport	___Mortuary Record	___Newspapers	___1790 ___1870
___Memorial Card	___Headstone	___Periodicals	___1800 ___1880
___Obituary	___Town/City History	___Biographies	___1810 ★ 1890
___Photographs		___Genealogies	___1820 ___1900
___School Records	**County Records**	___Local Histories	___1830 ___1910
___Work Records	___Civil Court Record	___Yearbooks	___1840 ___1920
___Pension Records	___Criminal Record	___Trade Journals	___1850 ___1930
___Financial Records	___Divorce Record	___Business Records	___1860 ___1940
___Health Records	___Guardianship Record		
___Insurance Records	___Deed/Mortgage Record	*The above checklist of sources*	
___Licenses	___Probate/Estate Record	*is by no means comprehensive!*	
___Scrapbook	___County History		

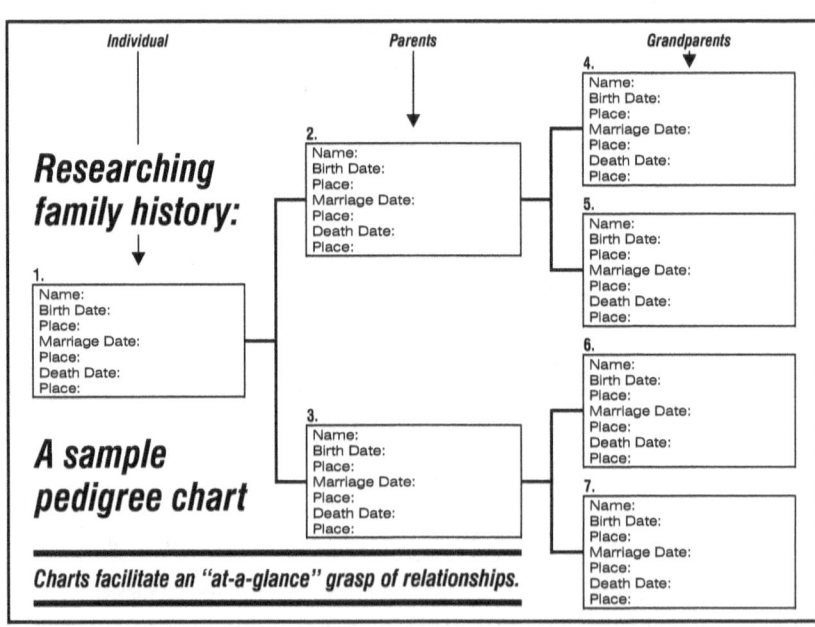

Researching family history:

A sample pedigree chart

Charts facilitate an "at-a-glance" grasp of relationships.

Appendix III: Source Citation 101

Source Citation 101 compares citation formats of the *Chicago Manual of Style* (17th ed., 2017), the *MLA Style Manual* (8th ed., 2016), and *Evidence Explained: Citing History Sources from Artifacts to Cyberspace*, by Elizabeth Shown Mills (3rd ed., 2017).

Source citations defined. Citations identify, in consistent detailed form, the source(s) for a particular assertion in a text. Source citations include footnotes/endnotes and bibliographic entries. Complete and accurate citations enable future researchers to verify your work.

Footnotes and endnotes. Footnotes/endnotes include the title, author, type of publication, publisher, publication place and date, and page number(s). Footnotes/endnotes may cite multiple sources for the same assertion, and may also include the author's analysis.

Bibliographies and source lists. Bibliographic entries include title, author, type of publication, publication place, and publication date. Entries do not document a particular fact like the footnote/endnote, but may include commentary (i.e. an "annotated bibliography").

Chicago Manual of Style. The 17th edition (2017) is as straightforward as ever. In the example provided, note the differences between bibliographic entries and footnotes/endnotes. For example, page numbers in articles are omitted from bibliographic entries.

Chicago Manual footnote/endnote:

Book: (1) Herkimer Oglethorpe. *My Lazy Life of Sloth, Indolence, and Redundancy.* (King of Prussia, Pa.: Petunia Press, 2014), pg. 577-579.

Article: (2) Hiram Fizzwater, "Fifty Ways to Mow the Front Lawn," *The Artful Yard Man* (Summer 2016): 9-12. (Deep Valley, N.Y.: Deep Publications, 2016).

Website: (3) Mundo Millflap, "Beatnik on the Bongos: Greenwich Village in the 1950s," accessed June 5, 2018, *https://www.coolcat.hip/BeatBongos.html.*

Chicago Manual bibliographic entry:

Book: Oglethorpe, Herkimer. *My Lazy Life of Sloth, Indolence, and Redundancy.* King of Prussia, Pa.: Petunia Press, 2014.

Article: Fizzwater, Hiram. "Fifty Ways to Mow the Front Lawn," *The Artful Yard Man*, Summer 2016. Deep Valley, N.Y.: Deep Publications, 2016.

Website: Millflap, Mundo, "Beatnik on the Bongos: Greenwich Village in the 1950s." Accessed June 5, 2018. *https://www.coolcat.hip/BeatBongos.html.*

MLA Style Manual. The 8th edition (2016) simplified bibliographic citation. Punctuation fussiness was dialed back, so now only commas and periods are used. Curiously, the place of publication is no longer required. MLA style allows footnotes, but prefers in-text citations.

MLA footnote/endnote:

Book: (1) Herkimer Oglethorpe. *My Lazy Life of Sloth, Indolence, and Redundancy.* (Petunia Press, 2014), 577-579.

Article: (2) Hiram Fizzwater, "Fifty Ways to Mow the Front Lawn," *The Artful Yard Man* (Summer 2016), pg. 9-12.

Website: (3) Mundo Millflap, "Beatnik on the Bongos: Greenwich Village in the 1950s," accessed June 5, 2018, *www.coolcat.hip/BeatBongos.html*.

MLA bibliographic entry:

Book: Oglethorpe, Herkimer. *My Lazy Life of Sloth, Indolence, and Redundancy.* Petunia Press, 2014.

Article: Fizzwater, Hiram. "Fifty Ways to Mow the Front Lawn," *The Artful Yard Man*, Summer 2016, pg. 9-12.

Website: Millflap, Mundo, "Beatnik on the Bongos: Greenwich Village in the 1950s." Accessed June 5, 2018. *www.coolcat.hip/BeatBongos.html*.

Evidence Explained. This recommended reference generally follows the format of the *Chicago Manual of Style*, with some simplifications. Most useful are examples for citing every kind of source. Also by Ms. Mills is *Citing Online Historical Sources Evidence Style* (2007).

Evidence Explained footnote/endnote:

Book: (1) Herkimer Oglethorpe. *My Lazy Life of Sloth, Indolence, and Redundancy.* (King of Prussia: Petunia Press, 2014), 577-579.

Article: (2) Hiram Fizzwater, "Fifty Ways to Mow the Front Lawn," *The Artful Yard Man*, Summer 2016, 9-12.

Website: (3) Mundo Millflap, "Beatnik on the Bongos: Greenwich Village in the 1950s." *https://www.coolcat.hip/BeatBongos.html* : accessed 5 June 2018.

Evidence Explained bibliographic entry:

Book: Oglethorpe, Herkimer. *My Lazy Life of Sloth, Indolence, and Redundancy.* King of Prussia: Petunia Press, 2014.

Article: Fizzwater, Hiram. "Fifty Ways to Mow the Front Lawn." *The Artful Yard Man*, Summer 2016, 9-12.

Website: Millflap, Mundo. "Beatnik on the Bongos: Greenwich Village in the 1950s." (*https://www.coolcat.hip/BeatBongos.html* : 2018).

Consistency is the aim. No matter what citation format you choose, even if you make up your own, apply it consistently throughout. Make it easy on the scholars bound to consult your work far into the future.

Bibliography

For those interested in further study of topics touched upon in this book, the following bibliography is presented by category, with entries within each category listed alphabetically by author. The categories are historiography; general history theory & practice; local history theory & practice; genealogy theory & practice; the craft of research; source citation; the craft of writing; and the author's works referenced in practical examples in this book. Books listed here for further guidance and enrichment have also served as dependable sources for the author's research and study, past and present.

Historiography

Bloch, Marc. *The Historian's Craft*. New York, N.Y.: Vintage Press, 1964.

Braudel, Fernand. *On History*. Chicago, Ill.: University of Illinois Press, 1982.

Ginzburg, Carlo. "Microhistory: Two or Three Things That I Know About It." *Critical Inquiry 20* (Fall 1993), Pgs. 10-35. Chicago, Ill.: University of Chicago Press, 1993.

Iggers, Georg G. *Historiography in the 20th Century: From Scientific Objectivity to the Postmodern Challenge*. Hanover, N.H.: University Press of New England, 1997.

Iggers, Georg G.; Wang, Q. Edward; and Mukherjee, Supriya. *A Global History of Modern Historiography*. London, England: Pearson-Longman, 2008.

Kagan, Donald. *Thucydides: The Reinvention of History*. Carlsbad, Calif.: Brecourt Academic, 2009.

Khaldun, Ibn. *The Muqaddimah: An Introduction to History*. (c. 1377; trans. from Arabic by Franz Rosenthal, 1958) Princeton Classics / Princeton University Press, 2015.

Luraghi, Nino. *The Historian's Craft in the Age of Herodotus*. New York, N.Y.: Oxford University Press, 2001.

Mabillon, Jean. *De re diplomatica* (1681). Translated from Latin by Richard Wertis as *On Diplomatics*, in *Historians at Work - Vol. II*. New York, N.Y.: Harper & Row, 1972.

Magnusson, Sigurour Gylfi, and Szijarto, István M. *What is Microhistory?: Theory and Practice*. New York, N.Y.: Routledge, 2013.

Ranke, Leopold von. *The Theory and Practice of History* (anthology of 19th-century writings; Georg G. Iggers and Konrad von Moltke, eds.). Indianapolis, Ind.: Bobbs-Merrill, 1973.

Stunkel, Kenneth R. *Fifty Key Works of History and Historiography*. New York, N.Y.: Routledge, 2011.

The Micro-Historian's Guide to
RESEARCH, EVIDENCE, & CONCLUSIONS *Bibliography*

General History Theory & Practice
Bailyn, Bernard. *Sometimes and Art: Nine Essays on History*. New York, N.Y.: Alfred A. Knopf, 2015.

Howell, Martha, & Prevenier, John. *From Reliable Sources: An Introduction to Historical Methods*. Ithaca, N.Y.: Cornell University Press, 2001.

Maza, Sarah. *Thinking About History*. Chicago, Ill.: University of Chicago Press, 2017.

Novick, Peter. *That Noble Dream: The "Objectivity Question" and the American Historical Profession*. Cambridge, England: Cambridge University Press, 1988.

Salivouris, Michael J., with Furay, Conal. *The Methods and Skills of History* (4th ed.). Hoboken, N.J.: Wiley-Blackwell, 2015.

Tosh, John. *The Pursuit of History: Aims, Methods, and New Directions in the Study of History* (6th ed.). New York, N.Y.: Routledge, 2015.

Trouillot, Michel-Rolph. *Silencing the Past: Power and the Production of History* (2nd ed.) Boston, Mass.: Beacon Press, 2015.

Tuchman, Barbara W. *Practicing History*. New York, N.Y.: Alfred A. Knopf, Inc., 1981.

Wineburg, Sam. *Historical Thinking and Other Unnatural Acts*. Philadelphia, Pa.: Temple University Press, 2001.

Local History Theory & Practice
Amato, Joseph A. *Rethinking Home: A Case for Writing Local History*. Berkeley, Calif.: University of California Press, 2002.

Archibald, Robert R. *A Place to Remember: Using History to Build Community*. Walnut Creek, Calif.: AltaMira Press, 1999.

Cauvin, Thomas. *Public History: A Textbook of Practice*. New York, N.Y.: Routledge, 2017.

Kammen, Carol. *On Doing Local History* (3rd. ed.). Lanham, Md.: AltaMira Press, 2014.

Kyvig, David E., and Marty, Myron A. *Nearby History: Exploring the Past Around You* (3rd. ed.). Lanham, Md.: AltaMira Press, 2010.

Wilson, Amy H. (ed.). *Encyclopedia of Local History* (3rd ed.). Lapham, Md.: Rowman & Littlefield, 2017.

Genealogy Theory & Practice
Anderson, Robert Charles. *Elements of Genealogical Analysis*. Boston, Mass.: New England Historic Genealogical Society, 2014.

The Board for Certification of Genealogists. *Genealogy Standards*. Orem, Utah: Ancestry Publishing, 2014.

Greenwood, Val D. *The Researcher's Guide to American Genealogy (4th Ed.)*. Baltimore, Md.: Genealogical Publishing Co., 2017.

Jacobus, Donald Lines. *Genealogy as a Pastime and Profession*. Baltimore, Md.: Genealogical Publishing Co., 1968.

Mills, Elizabeth Shown (ed.). *Professional Genealogy: A Manual for Researchers, Writers, Editors, Lecturers, and Librarians*. Baltimore, Md.: Genealogical Publishing Co., 2001.

Rose, Christine. The *Genealogical Proof Standard: Building a Solid Case*. San Jose, Calif.: CR Publications, 2005.

Stratton, Penelope L., and Hoff, Henry B. *Guide to Genealogical Writing* (3rd ed.). Boston, Mass.: New England Historic Genealogical Society, 2014.

The Micro-Historian's Guide to
RESEARCH, EVIDENCE, & CONCLUSIONS *Bibliography*

The Craft of Research

Anderson, Margo J. *The American Census: A Social History* (2nd ed.). New Haven, Conn.: Yale University Press, 2015.

Baker, Alan R. H. *Geography and History: Bridging the Divide*. Cambridge, England: Cambridge University Press, 2003.

Booth, Wayne C.; Colomb, Gregory G.; & Williams, Joseph M. *The Craft of Research*. Chicago, Ill.: University of Chicago Press, 2008.

Brundage, Anthony. *Going to the Sources: A Guide to Historical Research and Writing* (6th ed.). Hoboken, N.J.: Wiley-Blackwell, 2017.

Dollarhide, William, and Thorndale, William. *Map Guide to the U.S. Federal Census, 1790-1920*. Baltimore, Md.: Genealogical Publishing Co., 1987.

Houston, Brant. *The Investigative Reporter's Handbook: A Guide to Documents, Databases, and Techniques*. Boston, Mass.: Bedford-St. Martins, 2009.

Presnell, Jenny L. *The Information-Literate Historian: A Guide to Research* (3rd ed.). New York, N.Y.: Oxford University Press, 2018.

Source Citation

The Chicago Manual of Style (17th ed.). Chicago, Ill.: University of Chicago Press, 2017.

*MLA Style Manual and Guide to Scholarly Publishing (*8th ed.). New York, N.Y.: Modern Language Association of America, 2016.

Mills, Elizabeth Shown. *Evidence Explained: Citing History Sources from Artifacts to Cyberspace* (3rd ed.). Baltimore, Md.: Genealogical Publishing Co., 2017.

Mills, Elizabeth Shown. *QuickSheet - Citing Online Historical Resources - Evidence! Style*. Baltimore, Md.: Genealogical Publishing Co., 2007.

The Craft of Writing

The Associated Press Stylebook & Briefing on Media Law (50th ed.). New York, N.Y.: Associated Press, 2017.

Cappon, Rene. *The Associated Press Guide to News Writing: The Resource for Professional Journalists*. New York, N.Y.: Arco Publishing, 2000.

The Chicago Manual of Style (17th ed.). Chicago, Ill.: University of Chicago Press, 2017.

Clark, Roy Peter. *Writing Tools: 50 Essential Strategies for Every Writer*. New York, N.Y.: Little, Brown & Co., 2008.

Garner, Bryan A. *Garner's Modern American Usage*. New York, N.Y.: Oxford University Press, 2003.

Garner, Bryan A. *The Chicago Guide to Grammar, Usage, and Punctuation*. Chicago, Ill.: University of Chicago Press, 2016.

Merriam-Webster's Collegiate Dictionary (11th ed.). Springfield, Mass.: Merriam-Webster, 2003. [Chicago Manual of Style – and the author's – first-choice dictionary]

Strunk, William, Jr., and E. B. White. *The Elements of Style*. 4th ed. Boston, Mass.: Allyn and Bacon, 2000.

Truss, Lynne. *Eats, Shoots & Leaves: The Zero Tolerance Approach to Punctuation*. New York, N.Y.: Gotham Books, 2004.

Zinsser, William. *On Writing Well: The Classic Guide to Writing Nonfiction*. 7th ed. New York, N.Y.: Harper-Collins, 2006.

The Micro-Historian's Guide to
RESEARCH, EVIDENCE, & CONCLUSIONS   *Bibliography*

Works by the author referenced in practical examples throughout this book:
Bacon, Reginald W. *The Juggler's Manual of Cigar Box Manipulation & Balance.* Groveland, Mass.: Variety Arts Press, 1983.

_____ *The Juggler's Manual of Manipulative Miscellanea: The Classic Skills with Top Hat, Cane, Nesting Cups, & Assorted Objects.* Newburyport, Mass.: Variety Arts Press, 1984.

_____ (ed.). *The Middler.* [biannual journal of the Society of Middletown (Conn.) First Settlers Descendants]. Newburyport, Mass.: SMFSD, 2005-2018.

_____ *A Vaudeville Retrospective: American Vaudeville 1880-1930* (illustrated lecture, performance, and exhibition). 2008-present.

_____ "Historian of 20th-century entertainment tells the story of the New England 'trolley park'," *NEPA Exchange,* summer 2008. Manchester, Conn.: New England Park Association, 2008.

_____ *The Curator's Primer on American Vaudeville.* Newburyport, Mass.: Variety Arts Press, 2008.

_____ et al. Vaudeville history component of *Boston's Theatre History* (permanent exhibition at the Paramount Center, Boston, Mass.). Boston, Mass.: Emerson College, 2009.

_____ (ed.). "Native Americans in Middletown: Who called it 'home' before our 'First Settlers'?", part I & II, in *The Middler,* [biannual journal of the Society of Middletown (Conn.) First Settlers Descendants]. Newburyport, Mass.: SMFSD, spring & fall issues, 2010.

_____ *Just a Tot in Tannersville: The Recollections of a Railroad Avenue Boy on the Busy Summer Life of the 1950s.* Newburyport, Mass.: Variety Arts Press, 2008, 2011.

_____ *A Micro-History of the Tannersville Four-Corners.* Newburyport, Mass.: Variety Arts Press, 2011.

_____ *Early Families of Middletown, Conn. - Vol. I: 1650-1654.* Newburyport, Mass.: Variety Arts Press, 2012.

_____ *The Cranky Typographer's Book of Major Annoyances: Helpful Graphics Tips for Do-It-Yourself Designers.* Newburyport, Mass.: Variety Arts Press, 2014.

_____ *The Cranky Editor's Book of Intolerable Fox Paws (Oops! Faux Pas!): Helpful Writing & Style Tips So You Won't Look Stoopid.* Newburyport, Mass.: Variety Arts Press, 2014.

_____ *The Wesley H. Bacon Reader: Pursuits, Passions, & Peregrinations of a 20th-Century Autodidact.* Newburyport, Mass.: Variety Arts Press, 2015.

_____ *The Visitor's Guide to the Weeks Brick House & Gardens.* Newburyport, Mass.: Variety Arts Press, 2015.

_____ "The 'Case' of the Banjo-Mandolin," *Variety Arts Gazette,* winter 2016 & winter 2017. Newburyport, Mass.: Variety Arts Press, 2016-2017.

_____ *Vintage From Vinyl: Early Recordings of the Goodtime Ragtime Vaudeville Revival.* Newburyport, Mass.: Variety Arts Press, 2017.

_____ *The HABS and the HABs NOTS: Documenting the Architecture of Newburyport in the Historic American Buildings Survey.* Newburyport, Mass.: Variety Arts Press, 2017.

_____ *Chauncey Richmond & "The Old Buckbee": The Story of a Banjo, Its Maker, and Its Player.* Newburyport, Mass.: Variety Arts Press, 2018.

Index

Abbott, Lynn, 9
acrobatics, 34
Adams House hotel (Boston, Mass.), 66
Aisne-Marne American Cemetery (France), 89
Albee, E. F., 66
Alexander, Michael, 88
Allis, Sam, 95
Alltagsgeschichte, 58, 60
American Assn. for State & Local History, 93
American Historical Association, 17
analytical model (of history writing), 75
Anderson, Robert Charles, 7, 9
Archibald, Robert R., 94
Arlen, Harold, 88
Arlington, Mass., 96
Armenian-American culture, 94, 96-97
Arnold, Edmund C., 9
apparently (proof level), 42

B. F. Keith's New Theatre (Boston, Mass.), 66
banjo, 14, 15, 18, 21, 33-34, 43, 45, 78-79, 85
banjo-mandolin, 88
Bailyn, Bernard, 9
Ballard, Martha, 6
baloney detector, 92, 94
Barnum, P. T., 66, 69
Barnum's American Museum (N.Y.), 66
BCG Genealogical Proof Standard, 41
Belleau Wood (France), 89-91
Benes, Peter, 9
Belin, Irving, 88
Berra, Yogi, 11, 24
bibliographies, 21-22, 28-29, 85, 103, 105-108
Bloch, Marc, 54
Booth, Wayne C., 7
Boston, Mass., 65-68
Boston Globe, 95
Boston (Mass.) Museum, 66
Bradbury, Eben, 89
Braudel, Fernand, 7, 9, 54, 57
Bronx, N.Y., 15, 33-34, 43, 45
Bronx (N.Y.) Historical Society, 21
Brooklyn (N.Y.) Daily Eagle, 23
Brooklyn (N.Y.) Historical Society, 21
Brooklyn (N.Y.) Public Library, 21
Bruno, Charles & Son, 45-46
Brynner, Yul, 97
Buckbee, George E., 33
Buckbee, John Henry I, 14, 15, 21, 33, 43-44, 45, 78, 79, 85
Buckbee, John Henry II, 33
Burke, James, 59

Cahill, Bill, 9
Canobie Lake Park (Salem, N.H.), 86
Cantor, Eddie, 88
Cap'n Crunch, 91
Cappon, Rene J., 82
Catskill Mountains (N.Y.), 8, 44, 87, 94-97
causality, 61-63
census research, 15, 18, 20, 21, 33, 35, 88, 94, 98, 100
Center for Media Literacy, 91
Centre for Microhistory Research, 60
certainly (proof level), 42
change, 61-62
Charlemagne, 45
Clearfield, Andrea, 88
Clearfield, Sam, 88
Colomb, Gregory G., 7
Colonial Revival, 66, 68-69, 93
conclusions, formulation of, 49-67
Connecticut Historical Society, 24
Connecticut Society of Genealogists, 24
Connecticut State Library (Hartford, Conn.), 24
contextual knowledge, 14, 93, 97
continuity, 61-62
Covert, Cathy, 9
Crane, Madilyn Coen, 82
credibility (of evidence), 38-39
Cullen, Frank, 9
"cultural history", 55
Cummings, Abbott Lowell, 9
Curran, Joan F., 82

Davis, Janet, 9
descriptive model (of history writing), 74
Devine, Donn. 7
dictionary, 42, 76
Dorau, Bethany Groff, 89
Drew University (Madison, N.J.), 60

Ebay, 88
editing, 84-85
Elka Park (Tannersville, N.Y.), 97
Embargo Act of 1807, 68
Emerson College (Boston, Mass.), 65-68, 69
Evers, Alf, 9
Evidence, Concepts in the Evaluation of, 36
evidence, deriving facts from, 39
evidence, evaluation of, 36-47
evidence, primary, 37
evidence, derivative/secondary, 38
evidence, direct, 38
evidence, indirect, 38

facts (derived from evidence), 39
family group sheet, 99, 101
"Fiji Mermaid" (at the Boston Museum), 66
footnotes, 16, 21-22, 28-29, 85, 101-102

Garner, Brian, 82
Garvin, James L., 9
genealogist's toolkit, 99-100
genealogy, 6, 7, 8, 9, 32, 41, 42, 60, 82, 99-102
Gershwin, George, 88
Gershwin, Ira, 88

Gillis, Andrew J. "Bossy", 35
Ginzburg, Carlo, 6, 48, 56, 57, 59, 61
Girouard, Nicki, 9
Gibbon, Edward, 53
Godfrey Memorial Lib. (Middletown, Conn.), 24
Goodman, Benny, 88
Gotham Center for New York City History, 21
Gottlieb, Jack, 88
Greenland, N.H., 15, 78, 80
Greenwood, Val D., 7

Hemenway, Abby, 9
Herodotus, 7, 52
historical/diplomatics mode (of proof), 40
History Writer's Checklist, 68
Hobhouse, Henry, 59
Hobsbawm, Eric, 54
Hoff, Henry B., 82
historiography, 52-59
Hollywood, 66, 69
Howell, Martha. 7, 62
Hyanno, Mary (Wampanoag princess), 63

Iggers, George C., 59, 60
improvisation, 32-33
information gathering, 27-28
inquiry, formulating, 13
International Jugglers' Association, 19
Ives, Dr. Timothy, 64

Jacobus, Donald Lines, 7, 9, 54
jazz, 88
Jolson, Al, 88
juggling, 34

Kammen, Carol, 7, 9, 94
Kawanui, Kehaulani, 64
Keith, B. F., 66
Keith Memorial Theatre (Boston, Mass.), 67
Kenyon, Paul, 9
Kern, Jerome, 88
Kerr, Deborah, 97
Khaldun, Ibn, 7, 53
Kimball, Moses. 67
King and I, The (1956 movie), 97
Klarfeld, Isaac, 88
knowledge, limits of, 50-52
Kurlansky, Mark, 6, 48
Kyvig, David E., 94

Labaree, Benjamin W., 69
Lasser, Michael, 88
Lavin, Dr. Lucianne, 64
Lawrence, Gertrude, 97
legal/deductive model (of proof), 40
Lebvre, Lucien, 54
Leclerc, Michael J., 82
Levi, Giovanni, 48, 56, 57
Library of Congress, U.S.
   (Washington, D.C.), 17, 23, 35

likely (proof level), 42
Lion/Melodeon/Gaiety/Bijou Theatre, 66
Lincoln, Abraham, 24
Lincoln Park (Dartmouth, Mass.), 88
Lincoln Park (Norwich, Conn.), 19
local historian's toolkit, 94
local history, 93-98, 100
Lomas, Robert I. Jr., 33-34
Lomas, William B. ("Will Lyle"), 33
Lomas, Marion Ward, 33
Ludtke, Alf, 48. 58, 59, 60
Luebking, Sandra Hargraves, 100

Mabillon, Dom Jean, 7, 53
Magnusson, Sigurdur Gylfi, 48, 60
Marty, Myron A., 94
McCullough, David, 7, 13
media literacy, 8, 93
Michelet, Jules, 53
microhistory, 5, 55-61
Microhistory, Principles of 21st-Century, 48
Middlesex County Historical Society
   (Middletown, Conn.), 24
Middletown, Conn., 14, 24, 63-64
Middler, The, 24
Mills, Elizabeth Shown, 7, 8, 9, 21, 31,
   74, 85, 99-100, 103, 104
Mizuhara, Gintaro ("M. Gintaro"), 34
Montandon, Roger, 19
Mountain Park (Holyoke, Mass.), 86
Museum of the City of New York Archives, 21

narrative model (of history writing), 75
Nazi era (in Germany), 58, 60-61
Neithammer, Lutz, 58, 60
NEPA Exchange, 86
Newburyport, Mass., 68-69, 89
Newburyport (Mass.) Preservation Trust, 68
New England Historic Genealogical Soc., 82
New England Park Association, 86
"new left history", 55
"new social history", 5
New York City Library of the Perf. Arts, 23
New York Historical Society, 21
New York City Municipal Archives, 21
New York Public Library, 21
New York Clipper, 23
New York State Archives, 21
Newburyport, Mass., 15, 35
Newton, L. J., 9
Nixon, Marni, 97
Norman Conquest, 45
Norwich (Conn.) Bulletin, 19
Norwich, Conn., 19
Norwich & Westerly Railway Co., 19
nostalgia, 95-96

objectivity, 50-52, 68, 86-87
O'Brien, Jean M., 63
Olin Library (Wesleyan University), 24

The Micro-Historian's Guide to
RESEARCH, EVIDENCE, & CONCLUSIONS   Index

O'Neil, Gary, 64
Onteora Park (Tannersville, N.Y.), 97
Orpheum Theatre (Tannersville, N.Y.), 97
outline & organization, 76-78
outline, topic-based. 76-77
outline, sentence-based, 76-77
outline, preliminary "mind-map", 76-77

Pain, Wellesley, 34
Paramount Center (Boston, Mass.), 65-68
pedigree chart, 99, 102
perspective, 93, 97
Philadelphia, Pa., 88
plausibly (proof level), 42
postmodernist history, 55, 61
"practical problem" (vs. research problem), 14
Prevenier, Walter, 7, 62
probably (proof level), 42
proof, 39
proof levels, 42-43
proof standards, 39-40
proofreading, 85
puritanism, 24, 64, 66

Quassy Park (Middlebury, Conn.), 86

Ranger, T. O., 54
Ranke, Leopold von, 7, 53
Rawlings, Elden, 9
Register, The (NEHGS), 76
relevance (of evidence), 38
reliability (of evidence), 38
"research problem" (vs. practical problem), 14
Research Checklist (individual), 102
research execution, 27-35
Research Extract Form, 30
Research Log, 29, 100
research planning, 11-25
Research Execution Checklist, 26
Research/Evidence/Conclusions Flow Chart, 10
Revere, Paul, 96
Richmond, Chauncey, 18, 44, 78, 79, 85
Ricketts, John Bill, 66
Rip Van Winkle Lake (Tannersville, N.Y.), 96
Riverside Park (Agawam, Mass.), 86
Rodda, Anne, 59-60
Russell Library (Middletown, Conn.), 24
Russia, 88, 96
Rybczynski, Witold, 59

"**S**hall We Dance" (song), 97
serendipity, 32-33, 89-90
Seroff, Doug, 9
Scandella, Domenica ("Menocchio"), 6
scientific method (of proof), 41
Shaw, Arnold, 9
slavery, 68-69
Slout, William, 9
SMFSD [Middletown (Conn.) Settlers Desc.], 63
Source Documentation Form, 22

sources, documenting, 21-22, 28-31, 85, 103-104, 105-108
sources: primary, secondary, & tertiary, 16
sources, surveying & prioritizing, 15-18
Spieldenner, Sharon, 9
Standage, Tom, 59
Stern, Isaac. 65
Stewart, George R., 6, 48
Strand Magazine, 34
Stratton, Penelope L., 82
Strunk, William, Jr., 82
stylebook, 82, 83, 84, 85
substance, 38
summary narrative, 73-90
summary narrative, conceiving, 73-74
summary narrative, writing, 82
Szucs, Loretto Dennis, 100

Tannersville, N.Y., 13, 44, 87, 94-97
Taylor, Alan, 48, 54
Temple University (Philadelphia, Pa.), 88
test readers, 84
Thayer, Stuart, 9
Thucycides, 7, 53
Time Magazine, 35
Tosh, John, 32-33, 50-52, 75-76
Tremont, Bronx, N.Y., 34, 43, 45
"triangle trade", 69
trolley parks, 86
Tuchman, Barbara, 7, 9
Tucker, Sophie, 88

Ulrich, Laurel Thatcher, 6, 9, 48, 55

Variety (showbusiness newspaper), 23
Variety Arts Gazette, 88
vaudeville, 19, 21, 23, 44, 65-68, 78, 81, 86
"Vaudeville Retrospective, A", 23, 78, 81
vital records, 20, 99
Voltaire, 53

Wangunk tribe (Conn.), 63-64
Weeks Brick House (Greenland, N.H.), 15, 78, 80
Wertheim, Frank, 9
Wesleyan University (Middletown, Conn.), 64
West Indies trade, 70-71
Whalom Park (Lunenburg, Mass.), 86
White, E. B., 82
White, Loring H., 9
Wilmeth, Don B., 9
Williams, Joseph M., 7
World War One, 89-91
Wray, John H., 82
writer's toolkit, 82

Yale University Indian Papers Project, 63

Zinsser, William, 82

About the Author

Reginald W. Bacon is a museum and history professional with specialties in 17th- and 18th-century New England architecture and domestic life – and early 20th-century American popular music, vaudeville, and circus.

His first career as a journalist, editor, and publication designer informs his current work for museums and historic sites. His 35-year career as an acrobatic juggler/unicyclist, comedy dancer, and jazz/ragtime musician informs his performing arts research. For many of those years he worked in dazzling synchrony with a stellar juggling partner – his wife L.J. Newton. In all pursuits from publications to performance, he had the good fortune to encounter and learn from the finest mentors in their respective fields.

In addition to articles and books on local, regional, and topical history, his research and museum work includes developing interpretive materials for historic sites; collections management projects; professional conference presentations; private research consultations; the Smithsonian/National Endowment for the Humanities conference on the future of the American circus; and an illustrated lecture presentation, performance, and exhibition – exclusively for museums, libraries, and colleges – on the theatrical, economic, and cultural history of American vaudeville.

A graduate of Syracuse (N.Y.) University (B.A., Journalism, Newhouse School of Public Communications; B.A., Sociology, Maxwell School of Public Affairs) and Harvard (C.M.S., Museum Studies), R.W. Bacon is the author of a dozen books on varied history and performing arts topics. Forthcoming is *The Curator's Guide to American Vaudeville 1880-1930*.

R.W. Bacon and his wife, L.J. Newton, live in Newburyport, Mass., a small city north of Boston where the Merrimack River meets the Atlantic Ocean.

www.ingramcontent.com/pod-product-compliance
Lightning Source LLC
Chambersburg PA
CBHW030147240426
43672CB00005B/300